Enhancing Your
Presentation Skills

Praise for Till K. Kahrs and "Enhancing Your Presentation Skills"

"Till Kahrs has it exactly right! 'Enhancing Your Presentation Skills' has made a real difference in the effectiveness of NetCom Technologies' management teams. Our leaders are producing unprecedented results thanks to clearer communication and improved working relationships. Kahrs has given us a thoughtful, powerful guide for leaders at all levels to achieve a massive agenda for success."

Mario Avarez, AIA
Chairman/CEO
NetCom Technologies, Inc.

"'Enhancing Your Presentation Skills' is an excellent book that demystifies the art of public speaking. It's filled with a wealth of information and easy to understand techniques that definitely make presenting easier. I only wish Till's book had been available when I first ran for public office."

Christina Shea
Mayor
City of Irvine

"Till's very comprehensive presentation skills book is a real breath of fresh air. It's easy to understand, the skills that he teaches really work, and I've personally been able to benefit from applying the concepts in this book. I would highly recommend 'Enhancing Your Presentation Skills' to anyone who makes presentations in public. It's helped me present cases in court and it's definitely worthwhile reading!"

Joseph P. Spirito, Jr.
Partner McGaughey & Spirito

"I recommend that candidates for public office at all levels of government use this public speaking tool. It is insightful, entertaining, and all of the concepts Till Kahrs presents in 'Enhancing Your Presentation Skills' are right on target. Till shares his vast knowledge of this subject matter skillfully with his readers. Well done!"

Frank Caterinicchio
Political Consultant
Washington, DC

"'Enhancing Your Presentation Skills' is a clear and concise book on public speaking. Till's personable style makes for enjoyable reading. Using his techniques will help reduce the anxiety so many of us experience while giving presentations as well as improve our self-confidence. I would highly recommend Till's book and have done so to many clients who are involved in the corporate world."

Mitchell Shaffer, Ph.D.
Psychotherapist for the past 20 years

"Till effectively shares his extensive speaking experience in an easy to read book on presentation skills. As a public speaker myself, with a degree in the subject, I can state that the book is comprehensive and covers all aspects of effective presentations. There are a wide array of techniques and methods designed for immediate, practical application. Till knows where the rubber meets the road with respect to presentation skills. I have personally benefited from my interaction with Till. His knowledge in many areas of business and leadership has helped me professionally."

Paul N. Deputy, Ph.D., CCC-SLP
Dean, College of Education and Human Service Professions
Professor of Communication Sciences and Disorders
University of Minnesota Duluth

"'Enhancing Your Presentation Skills' is definitely a book to be shared. The information is extremely practical and relevant. Till has synthesized a mountain of knowledge and experience into a usable, valuable, 'quick read' resource tool. I would highly recommend it for both novice and expert speakers. I will certainly keep it close to my desk."

Regina Fink Ph.D. RN
Pain Management Consultant and Lecturer

"Anyone who values the ability to effectively communicate should read this book. 'Enhancing Your Presentation Skills' is concise and informative while offering powerful and effective techniques. I found myself incorporating Till's methods into my presentation the very next day…and I got the order!"

Jerry M. Baker
National Sales Manager
Napa Valley Winery

"'Enhancing Your Presentation Skills' by Till Kahrs contains very effective insights on the art and science of public speaking. The ideas and concepts presented in this book go beyond subjective theories, and place the subject matter into the arena of usefulness and practicality. This book has enhanced my ability and confidence to communicate ideas and concepts in a group environment."

Carl W. Rizzo, CPA
Board of Directors/CFO
The Cyberbuck Corporation

"After several years of public speaking, I found this book very helpful. Till has a great understanding of the needs of an audience, and very effectively instructs the reader on the best practices for making a presentation. His many examples of audience reaction to various speaking techniques made me chuckle with agreement. Thank you Till for the changes I plan to make in my own presentation skills."

Christine B. Hagan, Psy.D.
Licensed Psychologist

Enhancing Your Presentation Skills

Till K. Kahrs

Writers Club Press
San Jose New York Lincoln Shanghai

Enhancing Your Presentation Skills

Writers Club Press
an imprint of iUniverse.com, Inc.

For information address:
iUniverse.com, Inc.
620 North 48th Street, Suite 201
Lincoln, NE 68504-3467
www.iuniverse.com

ISBN: 0-595-12481-X

Printed in the United States of America

DEDICATION

This book would not be possible without the love and support of my dear Mother Ilse who is a saint in my eyes and the strongest and wisest person I've ever met. This book is dedicated to you!

Acknowledgements

There are several people that I'd like to thank for helping me with this book.

Thanks to Dr. Maurice Conway for his expert guidance and help with editing this project. My thanks to both Doug Jefferys and Maragaret Medlin for their assistance. I'd also like to thank my father, Dr. Karl H. Kahrs, for taking the time to review this book at its very early stages.

Also, there are so many wonderful trainers out there, too numerous to mention, from whom I've learned and continue to learn so much. Thanks as well to all of the great audiences that I have worked with.

Finally, thanks to all of you who have helped, supported, and encouraged me while I have been writing this book. I couldn't have done it without you!

Author's Note

This book is a comprehensive look at the subject of presentation skills based on my experience. I've traveled from Indiana to India giving seminars on this subject and I will share with you as much as I can about what I've learned.

Roughly half of the seminars that I currently teach have to do with enhancing presentation skills and the other half deal with business communication skills; specifically sales, negotiating, hiring, managing, telephone skills, and business writing.

As an added bonus, I've included an extra section at the end of this book called, "An Introduction to the 'Consultative Toolbox Technique'". This section will give you an overview of some dialogue skills that lie at the heart of the other courses offered by my company, Kahrs Communication Concepts. As you will see, these skills are powerful and also have an application to presentation skills.

To get the full value from any section in this book, it is advisable that you consider actually taking a class from Kahrs Communication Concepts. Whether it's changing physical behavior or adjusting verbal skills, "trying it" and "doing it" is truly the only way that we learn.

CONTENTS

Part One
Before We Get Started 1
    Foreword 3
    The Number One Fear That People Have 5
    Why Me, and How Did I Get Started? 6
    The Scariest Moment of My Life 7
    Just Trying It 11
    Coaching 12

Part Two
Physical Skills 13
    Eye Contact, Pausing, and Slowing Down 15
    Lock, Talk, and Pause 20
    Is Looking Good Really That Important? 24
    Energizing Your Presentation! 30
    Balancing Your Stance 31
    Gestures 32
    Smiling and an Open Face 38
    Voice Inflection and Volume 39
    Warming Up Your Voice 41

Part Three
Content and Organization 43
    Content and The Audience (It's About Them) 45
    Organization 48

The Organizational Outline *49*
The "Grabber" *49*
Problem/Opportunity *52*
Solution/Recommendation *52*
Support with Evidence *53*
Benefits to the Audience *56*
Call to Action/Next Steps *57*
Ending with A "Bang" *58*
How Long Should Your Presentation Be? *59*
Transitions *60*
Are You In The Know, and Do You Know Where You Are? *61*
Humor and Jokes *62*

Part Four
Visuals *65*
Designing Visuals *67*
Delivery with Visuals *71*
Absorb, Align, and Address *72*

Part Five
Odds and Ends *77*
Hi-Tech Presentations *79*
Pointers Of Any Kind Aren't Necessary *80*
Podiums *82*
Microphones *82*
Physical Skills in Different and Smaller Settings *84*
Handouts and Props *85*
Overheads and Projectors *86*
Flip Charts *87*
Reading A Script and Using Teleprompters *89*
Alternatives to Visuals, Scripts, and Teleprompters *94*
A Word about Preparation *96*

Speaking On the Spot *98*

How to Practice *101*

Dress *102*

What's The Best Time of Day to Present? *105*

The Day of the Event *105*

Beforehand and Loosening-Up *109*

Introductions *110*

Part Six

Questions and Answers 113

Why Is This So Tough? *115*

Getting Off On the Right Foot *115*

1) Raise Hand and Ask for Questions *117*

2) Select Someone and Listen *118*

3) Rephrasing/Repeating (Optional) *120*

4) Answer and Tie Back *122*

Should You? *123*

What Ifs *125*

Part Seven

Media Relations 131

Close-ups *133*

Epilogue *140*

Part Eight (Bonus Section)

An Introduction to the "Consultative Tool Box Technique" 143

Preface *145*

Who Is This About Anyway? *150*

Opening the Dialogue *151*

Active Listening *154*

Finding Out More *156*

Psychologist or Private Eye? *160*

Open-Ended Questions *162*
Handling Questions and Objections *166*
Recommending/Proposing *171*
Closing the Sale *173*
What Now? *175*
A Final Thought *175*

Part One

Before We Get Started

Foreword

Recent studies by Stanford University and AT & T suggest that your presentation skills and how you are perceived while making a presentation impact your career and upward mobility more than anything else does.

I've probably taught public speaking skills to over 100,000 people in the last 10 years. In that time I've also given over 2,000 speeches/seminars of various kinds. What I've learned is to expect the unexpected and to never underestimate your audience.

Even from someone who is experienced, the first few seconds in front of a fresh audience are crucial and in today's fast paced world, you don't have much time to grab your audience and hold its attention.

The fact that maybe you've done it before does not interest anyone, so like a professional golfer, you have to prove yourself each round, each tournament, on each new course. You may have a good track record, but what you did last weekend won't carry you through today. You're only as good as your last performance, and public speaking is performance art.

On the other hand, making a mistake or two and not being perfect won't be fatal. The last person beheaded after he spoke in public was, I believe, Sir Thomas More. It's probably not going to happen again anytime soon.

Audiences forgive and don't expect anyone to be infallible. It's when speakers panic and openly fall apart that things start getting considerably worse for the presenter.

Don't take yourself too seriously. And if something does go wrong, roll with it and then forget about it. It'll soon be forgotten anyway.

There's a great saying in the German language: "Es kann nicht den Kopf kosten"(Literally: It won't cost your head, but closer to 'it's not gonna' kill you'). Think to yourself like Gloria Gaynor sings, "I will survive," and you will.

So why this book and what's in it for you? Very simply, I'm passionate about this subject, I think that I know a little bit about it, and I want to help people with something that many studies consider to be the number one fear that people have.

In addition, enough people have inquired about "my book" after a seminar or speech, that writing one seemed like the natural thing to do.

What Are You Most Afraid Of?

Speaking Before a Group	41%
Heights	32%
Insects & Bugs	22%
Financial Problems	22%
Deep Water	22%
Sickness	19%
Death	19%
Flying	18%

Source: *The Book of Lists*

The Number One Fear That People Have

Years ago I was watching the TV show Seinfeld, which of course has now been relegated to permanent rerun status, and during this particular episode, Jerry and friends were talking about public speaking being the number one fear and that people fear it even more than dying. So someone on the show makes the comment, "You mean people would rather be in the box, than give the eulogy?"

Funny, but true. And no one is immune to this fear. Mark Twain once said, "There are two types of speakers, those that are nervous and those that are liars."

But, why do people become afraid when speaking in public?

I suppose no one knows for sure, we can only guess. Since I've been working in the field for over 10 years, my guess would be that public speaking amplifies people's insecurities.

We as humans all have fears and insecurities. It's natural, and our fears help us in many cases survive and overcome tremendous obstacles. Everyone has heard stories about the wonders of adrenaline and how mothers have had the strength to lift up cars to rescue their newborns.

But when you stand naked (meant figuratively of course) before a group of strangers it compounds all of our worst fears into one big moment of terror. We feel exposed, we feel as though we can't hide (that's why people love podiums by the way), and we're mortified in front of a room full of listeners.

To the audience, however, it rarely looks as bad as we actually feel.

Nevertheless, in the time that I've been consulting on this subject, I have seen the smartest and most successful individuals virtually brought to their knees.

Speaking in public can in many ways be a great equalizer because no matter how smart or rich you are, it won't help you when you hear your heart pounding and feel your mouth going dry. Absolutely no one is immune to what can happen to you on the platform.

Many great performers are nervous before a performance. Barbara Streisand is notorious for her stage fright, and so is Michael Jackson. Garth Brooks once said, "If I ever stop getting nervous before a perform-ance, it's time for me to quit."

Perhaps you can learn to harness your nervousness, control it, and use it to your advantage?

Why Me, and How Did I Get Started?

A lot of people ask me how or why I got into public speaking/training, and that's a hard one to answer.

My parents claim that when I was around 1 or 2, I used to enjoy bab-bling about in mindless baby talk to imaginary audiences in our modest backyard in Monterey, California. I apparently used gestures, some voice inflection, and eye contact. You could argue that I was born to speak, or a psychologist might suggest that I was reaching out to others, since I am an only child.

I do know that early on in grade school I always looked forward to giv-ing oral reports when most of the others in school dreaded the task. It was always rather fun for me, and I enjoyed it immensely.

After college, I spent 12 successful years in corporate sales and finally left the business world to try my luck at entertainment. It was a dream that I had suppressed for a long time, but now felt at last was time to pursue.

Because I had no illusions about "making it" in show business, I wanted to keep a day job and started communication skills consulting on a part time basis. Two European Country Top Ten Hits and several TV commercials and TV shows later, I decided to pursue consulting and training full-time.

But as I mentioned earlier, no one is immune to the perils of public speaking and although I think I'm pretty good, I was very humbled back in 1994.

The Scariest Moment of My Life

My musical career began to take-off overseas. I landed a few self-penned "hits" on European Radio, and after one of my songs hit the charts in Europe, I had to prepare myself for bigger venues to support an upcoming summer long promotional tour overseas.

It was in the spring of '94 that I ended up having lunch at the old Crazy Horse Steak House in Santa Ana, California. This club had been host to some of the biggest acts in Country Music including Garth Brooks, Billy Ray Cyrus, Pam Tillis and legends like Johnny Cash, Waylon Jennings, and Tammy Wynette.

I had been talking to then owner Fred Reiser about headlining a show there, and continued to remind him about the fan base that I had developed playing the local coffee house circuit for several years.

Typically, The Crazy Horse didn't allow local acts to do the headliner shows, but since I was receiving a lot of publicity in several newspapers and because my music had been played on several radio stations, I assured Mr. Reiser that I would pack the place, guaranteed.

Days before grabbing lunch at "The Horse", I had dropped off articles, promotional materials, and CDs for Mr. Reiser reminding him of "the buzz" that I had created relative to my impending European Tour.

Half way through lunch, Mr. Reiser came to my table unexpectedly and said, "Hey Till, I just got a call from Nashville this morning and one of our headliners had to cancel a show, can you do a show May 2 (which was only two weeks away)?"

I knew immediately that it would be next to impossible to put a band together and sell-out the place in that short a period of time, so I responded, "I'd love to!" Of course I also knew that I might never get a chance to headline a show again, so I took "the bird in hand" approach, even if it came with tremendous challenges.

After lunch I was very excited but at the same time terrified, as I thought to myself, "How am I going to do all of this?"

I put a band together in a few days, sold every ticket for the May 2 show, and even got some last minute press in local newspapers. It was an exciting time, but I was running on fumes.

What's even crazier is that two of the band members that I had originally hired for the show had to drop out in the last minute and I had to scramble for replacements. Keep in mind that my band had to learn all original material from scratch and that the show was now only days away.

Miraculously, I was able to pull together a second version of the band at the "eleventh hour" and we managed to get in one complete three-hour rehearsal. This was barely enough time to learn an entire catalogue of original material, even for the greatest of musicians.

On the day of the show, we did a sound check (this is when you load in your band's equipment and check microphone, mix, and sound levels). A typical sound check lasts about 15 minutes, no more than that, so after one hour, the guys in the sound booth were telling us, "Hey guys, that's fine, I think we've got it, see you tonight."

Pleading for extra much needed rehearsal time, I told the head sound engineer, "No problem, we'll be done in a second. We just have to figure out how this one song starts and how it ends because we've never played it before, ever."

The sound engineer was shocked, but let us continue rehearsing a few more moments. He certainly wasn't used to a comment like that from a headliner, yet imagine how I felt.

The reason I share this story is that I want you to know exactly what kind of pressure I was feeling. Even though this wasn't going to be a speech, it was still a presentation of sorts and I was scared out of my wits.

All of my closest friends, family, and fans were coming to see me at the world famous Crazy Horse. They had never seen me perform with a full band (steel guitar, lead guitar, rhythm guitar, bass, keyboards, and drums) and no one really knew how ill prepared the band and I actually were.

The hype surrounding this show had taken on a life of its own, and I was starting to feel the heat. More local articles appeared and the concert was mentioned on the two biggest country stations in southern California. Under no circumstances did I want to let anyone down.

Imagine this scenario. On the night of the show, I'm in the dressing room, waiting to walk on stage. The Crazy Horse is completely packed and getting restless. The band and I have never really performed together and I'm not even sure that I, or anyone else, can possibly remember the lyrics, chord changes, intros, and outros to 17 original songs that no one has ever heard before with a full band. All of this with only one rehearsal, now that's pressure!

The band was called on stage first, as I remained in the dressing room alone. I peered out the door at the crowd as the band members piled out. There were people everywhere and they were screaming. I have never been so absolutely scared in my life. I was completely terrified.

Thirty seconds before the local country disc jockeys, known as Max & Bryan, were to introduce me, one of the bouncers at The Crazy Horse informed me that there was someone from The LA Times there to review the show. "Great," I thought, "I will not only fail in front of my friends, family, and fans (and they might forgive me or at least feel sorry for me); but now I'll embarrass myself publicly and all of Los Angeles will know about my failure as well." PRESSURE!!! FEAR!!!

With about 15 seconds left before I am to walk on stage, I told myself, "Relax, what's the worst that can happen?" I tried to follow the lessons I had already learned from public speaking skills training; namely to focus in on one person at a time with my eyes and to burn off as much nervousness as possible by energizing my performance.

Max & Bryan called me out on stage and singing the first song had to be the hardest thing I've ever done. I don't even remember walking to the stage. I was extremely nervous, my knees were shaking, I felt faint, and at one time actually thought that I was going to pass out. BUT, I made it through the first song and by the third or fourth song I started to enjoy myself and have a little fun. By the time we played the last song, I didn't want to stop.

By focusing my eye contact on individual audience members, I was able to overcome my anxiety and harness the adrenaline flow, leading ultimately to a highly energized performance.

The show ended up being a hit with everyone and The LA Times reviewed my show on the front page of The Calendar section (the entertainment pages) with 2 photographs, one being color. This was an unusual occurrence for a local artist.

The review was quite favorable and one section of the article stated, "Throughout the evening, he (Till) connected to his fans with his easygoing charm. As much fun to watch as he was to listen to, he moved around the stage punctuating his music with energy that seemed to flow naturally."

It was a nice send-off to Europe and no one could have ever imagined how truly scared I had really been.

Being in public like that can be intimidating, frightening, and completely unpredictable. I know from personal experience.

I learned many things from acting and performing "live" in front of huge audiences. I spent the summer of '94 and '95 touring Europe with my band. I was probably the only country singer ever signed to a record label with an MBA.

What it means to you is that I combine my knowledge of business with performing and try to offer you the best of both worlds so that your business presentations have the pizzazz and appeal that will move audiences to take action and not change the channel on you. That's the bottom line!

Just Trying It

When I teach my seminars, many students don't want to be there quite frankly. Often times, participants are volunteered to go by their boss, or it's simply company policy, etc. They are afraid of speaking in public and many wouldn't be in my class if they weren't forced to go. This is what is commonly referred to as a "prisoner" in training circles.

One of the things that I always emphasize is that my participants should "shake hands with the snake". Face your fears and learn! I also remind everyone that it's O.K. to make mistakes, especially in a classroom environment.

The other point is that you cannot possibly learn anything, especially changing physical behavior, unless you actually expose yourself and try it. It reminds me of my first experience skiing.

I purchased a book through Sports Illustrated by Billy Kidd, an American Olympic Skier to help me prepare for my first ski trip when I was still in junior high school. It was a great book and I read it cover to cover several times and studied the photographs to prepare me for the slopes.

Interestingly enough, but not surprisingly, skiing was a lot different when I got off the chair lift and headed down the mountain. All that I had read and studied about seemed to be forgotten in an instant as I tried to avoid hurting myself. The book never mentioned how hard it was to simply get on and off the chair lift. That quickly became my number one fear.

Reading this book will give you an introduction to enhancing your presentation skills, but you have to actually try these techniques and practice them to have a chance to be successful in using them.

It's like riding a bike, really. It feels awkward at first, but it gets easier, and before you know it, you get really good at it. Embrace the challenge! Everyone gets "butterflies" before they speak. I do every time that I speak, and it helps me keep my edge. What you really need to do is learn how to make those butterflies fly in unison.

Ralph Waldo Emerson once said, "Do the thing you fear and the death of fear is certain." I think he was right.

Coaching

Right up front in the classes that I teach, I refer to myself as the coach. Good coaches don't embarrass anyone; they try to bring out the best in people. A coach, according to Webster's Dictionary, is an instructor or trainer. It is my belief also that a coach must be able to clearly demonstrate and model desired behaviors.

Just like in the National Football League and as with most professional sports, if the team has a losing record, the coach typically gets fired, not the players. I'd like to think that the pressure is on me to make you look good. You've got job security. Your company has sent you to me. Now I've got to make you look good. That's my job!

If this doesn't happen, I essentially lose my job and won't get referrals. Word travels fast and the training industry as a whole lives very much "word of mouth".

I've got some great plays designed for us to win, but I need you out on the field to execute this game plan, so that we both win.

I can't coach you when you're reading this book, though. But I can encourage you to try these concepts and skills that you learn. Hopefully I'll get the opportunity to work with you personally, but ultimately you'll be on your own anyway. If you learn to coach yourself, you'll be a step ahead of everyone else.

Finally, I always mention my "skills back guarantee". If you don't like your newfound skills (and I know you will), you can have your old skills back. That's my "skills back guarantee".

Part Two

Physical Skills

Eye Contact, Pausing, and Slowing Down

So the whole world's a stage, everyone's looking at you, your career is on the line, and you have nothing to say. Your mind goes blank. You knew what you were going to say, but now you forgot; and you fill the air with a big, "Uhhhhhhm!!!"

For many years now I've opened almost all of my presentation skills seminars by placing the participants one at a time in front of the classroom. I then have them speak briefly about some very familiar topics like what they do for a living and the most exciting thing that they are currently working on, etc. This sets the stage for the entire class.

I always stress before this exercise (which I refer to as a benchmark or baseline) starts that the participants should speak or present as they "normally would", and that there is no right or wrong to the exercise.

I add that a tennis pro usually wants to see your stroke before they start implementing changes. So at the beginning, I'm simply "checking their stroke" in a totally objective fashion. That helps relieve some of the anxiety.

I get the rest of the class to monitor specific objective physical and vocal behavior. I'll be covering the rest of the objective behavior in later sections, but one of the first things we observe on the physical side is eye movement.

Eye movement and eye contact is probably **the** most important component for the foundation of presentation skills. As you will see, handling eye contact properly is at the root of gaining composure and channeling your nervous energy.

Invariably, 95-100% of the students in my seminars scan the entire audience rapidly with their eyes during the benchmark exercise. As a consequence, the audience and everything in the room essentially becomes a complete blur to that participant because there is no point of focus.

Sometimes I joke with the audience and suggest that this particular individual was obviously looking at the ceiling for divine inspiration or perhaps at the walls or the floor for their notes. Either way, most speakers look rapidly around the room and incorporate what I call "aerosol eyes". In other words they spray the whole room with eye contact.

"Aerosol Eyes"

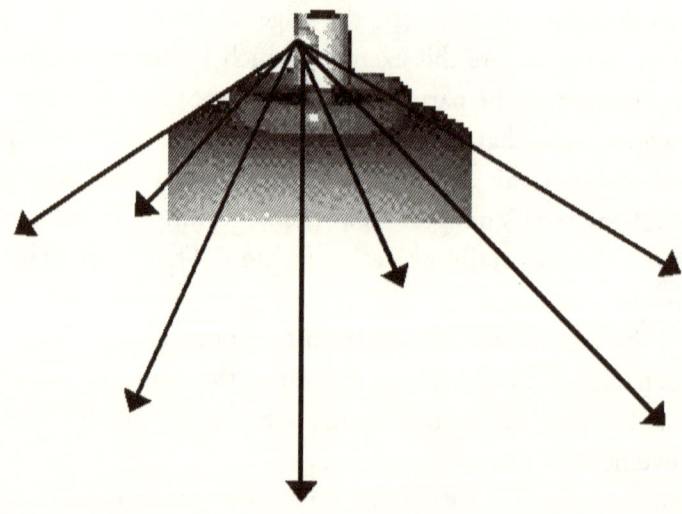

In my high school speech classes, that's also what they taught us to do. "Make eye contact with the audience, look at everyone". Many consultants even tell their clients to, "Just look at everyone". This represents a serious problem for the presenter and ultimately the audience.

Consider this, you are nervous as heck, especially at the beginning of any talk, your audience is sizing you up very quickly, and you react by moving your eyes rapidly around the room. This compounds the dilemma by making you even more anxious.

If you speed up your delivery and your eyes start darting around even more, while adrenaline is shooting through your body; things get worse. Scanning the room will overload your senses, cause you to fill the air with non-words, and undermine your ability to focus clearly. That's why so many speakers who are extremely confident beforehand, lose their train of thought once they get in front of an audience.

Perhaps you have experienced this very uncomfortable feeling yourself. But what is actually going on physiologically?

I'm not a physician, but let me explain it this way. If you've ever been in a car accident, you'll probably remember one thing about the sense of time. Time slowed down during the accident. Why? Because adrenaline is shooting through your body and when that happens, everything slows down; it's our body's way of preparing itself for a distressful situation.

Similarly, getting up in front of folks is scary, and the same thing happens to us. Public speaking makes us nervous and adrenaline starts charging through our bodies. Scanning the room rapidly makes matters worse, overloads our senses, and causes us to lose our train of thought because we're overwhelmed and not focused. As a consequence, everything slows down and we stand in front of a strange group of faces that are waiting anxiously to be inspired by us.

The problem is, when we forget what we're going to say, it seems like a lifetime to us, but it's only a few seconds time to the audience. Everyone is looking at us and we feel like an empty suit. And we always seem to lose our train of thought at exactly the wrong time.

After rehearsing your speech all night, and then finally approaching the front of the room the next day, you say to yourself, "I've got a photographic memory but it feels like I forgot to load the film again. Why does this always happen when I get up in front of a group of people to speak?"

Ironically, those few seconds pound slowly away like bell tolls in your head, when in actuality the audience feels it all in "real time". Because we're not used to this sudden burst of adrenaline (unless you're a cop or a race car driver) we are stunned and we then start to panic. Often times it's a straight downward spiral from there, and just like a real plane spiraling down towards the ground, it's so unnecessary and almost always preventable.

The key is to anticipate this adrenaline surge, learn to cope with it, keep focused, and slow down. But because we put pressure on ourselves for dialogue, and because our mind goes blank, we start to utter non-words (ahhhhhhs/uhhhhhhms) to fill in the empty space that makes us feel so uncomfortable.

In addition, we tend to look away from people when we can't think of what to say next. We look at the ceiling, at the floor, or continue to scan rapidly. The biggest "aaahhhaaa" is that we don't need to do that.

There is then, a direct link between "aerosol eyes" or the rapid scanning of the room, and pausing and slowing down your delivery. Pausing or saying absolutely nothing for a few seconds and focusing on only one person, is unquestionably no problem for the audience; in fact, it's a great way to keep the audience on their toes and interested. But for us, it feels very uncomfortable.

One of the things that I offer during my seminars or keynotes that gets a lot of laughs is, "I've never ever heard anyone say after someone's speech, 'That person sure paused a lot'". Interestingly enough however, if we use an endless number of non-words people will start counting them on scratch paper. They'll look at each other in the audience and snicker as the speaker does it again and again.

Keep in mind that (ahhhhhhs/uhhhhhhms) are not the only non-words that are out there. Frequently, people will say the same word over and over again, and that then essentially becomes their non-word.

For example when Moon Unit Zappa first came out with her satirical musical hit "Valley Girl", she spoofed and made fun of her generation always saying, "You know like", "I'm all", "I'm so sure", "No way".

Even professional speakers fall victim to this problem.

At a meeting that I attended in Detroit, Michigan, a major automotive manufacturer (I do a lot of consulting in the automobile industry) had hired a young lady to talk about marketing and market branding. She had fantastic credentials, her client list was most impressive, and she really knew what she was talking about, however, there was one little problem. While scanning the room rapidly with her eyes, she would say, "O.K.?" after every sentence, and then continue on with her rapid-fire delivery.

Now checking in with the audience for "buy in" is in principle not a bad idea, but saying "O.K.?" after literally every sentence was just a little too much to take. I, like many, started counting the number of times she said the word and stopped counting after approaching 100.

The point here is not that we should amuse ourselves counting the number of times speakers say the same word over and over again and rejoice in their nervousness, but rather to create an awareness that it's O.K. to pause and slow down, especially in a large group.

It's extremely effective as a matter of fact, but it sure feels unnatural when you're standing in front of people who have gathered to hear you speak. Remember though, no one has ever said of a speaker, "You know she just paused too much." It just doesn't happen.

I'd like to share a method with you that will help you slow down and pause.

When implemented properly, this technique will also assist you in eliminating non-words and please consider me to be "The Wizard of Ahhhhsssss" (one of my students affectionately came up with that one). Don't get stuck using the "Field of Dreams" approach relative to non-words, "I will talk and the words will come." Just pause and look at one person.

Don't say the first thing that comes to mind and don't move your mouth until you know exactly what you want to say! Don't say anything until the right words come. It's only a few seconds to your audience although it seems like a lifetime to you. Just pretend as though you're having a conversation with someone at lunch.

Lock, Talk, and Pause

So what can you do to get control of your eye movement and slow yourself down? Well, you could simply just close your eyes for a long time until you are more comfortable, but that's not realistic.

I highly recommend that you incorporate what I call the Lock, Talk, and Pause method. You lock in with one pair of eyes and talk only once you've firmly locked in (Lock). Once you've finished delivering that thought or sentence (Talk), move in silence (Pause) to another pair of eyes, and then start the process all over again.

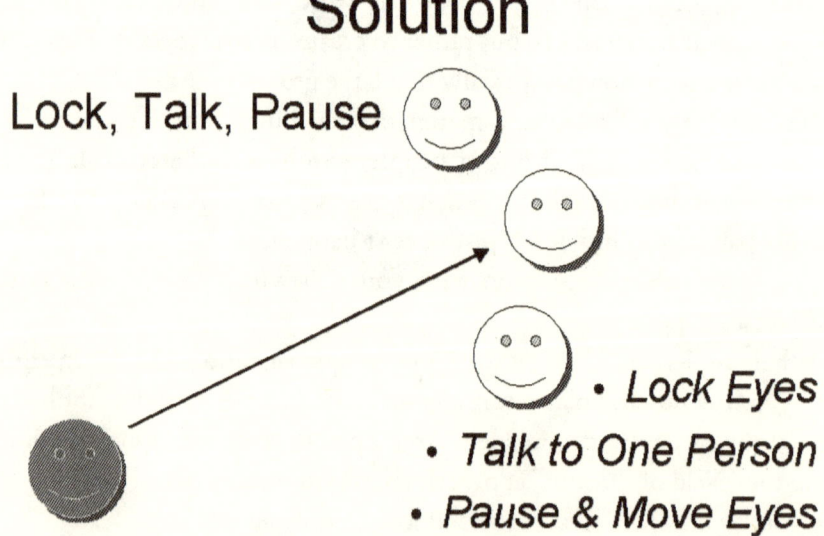

Solution

Lock, Talk, Pause

- Lock Eyes
- Talk to One Person
- Pause & Move Eyes

The most critical two things in this process are slowing down and pausing. Both are at the core of successfully executing Lock, Talk, and Pause. In my classes, when I teach this method, the first thing I tell students is, "You can't do this skill if you talk fast."

Fast talkers are the hardest ones to coach through something like this because they put so much pressure on themselves for dialogue. In other words, if you talk fast and lose your train of thought the chances of you using non-words become much higher.

Speaking quickly may also be perceived as being nervous or untrustworthy. Everyone has heard of a "fast talking salesman". Is that a positive or negative? And has anyone ever told you, "That speaker just didn't talk fast enough" or "That speaker was just to slow"? It won't happen.

The only person that I can think of who probably speaks too slow, is long time radioman, Paul Harvey. And he's made pausing and talking slow his signature, and bye golly, it works!

Initially most students of mine don't realize how important pausing and slowing down actually are. It's hard for people to understand sometimes, but after my classes are over I always get the same comments, year after year, "I didn't realize how important pausing was." "It sure makes it easier on me when I slow down". Slowing down and pausing takes the pressure off of you and makes it more comfortable for the audience to listen.

So, before you begin your presentation, walk up to the front of the room confidently, slowly, relax, pause, look at one person (Lock) and then speak (Talk) to that individual. After you "finish a thought" (sentence or group of words) with that person, stop talking (Pause) and in silence move your eyes to someone else, focus in, and do the same thing once again; Lock, Talk, and Pause.

What this does is give you an anchor and a point of focus in rough waters. This technique allows you to get into a natural rhythm. When you talk to one person at lunch, on the phone, or at the office, it's typically one to one. That's how most conversations take place. Do you lose your train of thought then? No, because you're speaking to one person at a time.

The Lock, Talk, and Pause method allows you to apply this same concept (speaking to one person at a time) to larger groups of people. Just speak to one person at a time, like you normally would, and you'll be fine. You're used to doing it anyway.

Incorporating this process also makes it easier for you to give an impromptu speech.

Armed with the Lock, Talk, and Pause skill method, you now have the power to deliver any conversation that you have at lunch with a friend to an entire room. It gives you the ability to speak to anyone, anytime, anyplace, anywhere without rehearsal as long as it's something you're familiar with. That's powerful and will forever change the way you view and handle public speaking!

Let's examine this method in detail and think about all the things that it accomplishes for you.

Invariably when I first introduce this technique, someone suggests that it feels strange to look people in the eye. My response to that is, "Well that may be, but in western culture eye contact is considered to be a positive thing." Having shifty eyes or refusing to make eye contact is considered to be suspect on almost every level.

Have you ever interviewed someone who did not make eye contact when answering important questions? I have, and it's creepy.

When a man proposes to a woman and he does not make eye contact as he tells her that he loves her, might the woman be skeptical? I think so. If I go to a car dealership to buy a used car and after inquiring about the authentic mileage of the car, the salesperson refuses to make direct eye contact with me and says, "Yea, those are original miles". Should I question his integrity?

Some old school presentation skills techniques suggest that you look at people's foreheads or pretend that the audience is naked (believe it or not). My only response would be, why? You've got enough to think about when presenting. Trying to mentally undress someone or looking at various body parts other than someone's eyes, doesn't really serve any purpose.

Obviously you don't ever want to stare at someone or make anyone feel uncomfortable. And some individuals aren't as receptive to eye contact as others. If that's the case, simply look at someone else first. Perhaps they'll feel more comfortable later.

But who should you look at first? Well, that doesn't actually matter. What does matter is that the audience thinks that your eye contact is completely random. There are no set rules here, but don't take the shooting gallery approach to eye contact; first this row and then that row.

Totally random is best, because you want to appear natural. You don't want people to think that you're trying out some kind of newly learned technique.

Can you use your eye contact to manage and even control the audience? Absolutely! But, don't glare at someone under any circumstances. You don't ever want to get into a confrontational mode with your audience (more about that later), but you can look at people, and pause; and that will serve to mange and control someone's lack of attention or restlessness.

Keep in mind also who your audience is. Is it your boss or someone who works for you? All these things will impact your decision on where to spread or hold the eye contact.

Sometimes what I do is look at people who I know are the naysayers or problem folks in the group early on. This way I let them know right away and it is if as I'm saying, "I'm aware of who you are and I am confident enough to look you right in the eye. You won't be able to throw me off." That deals with 99% of all problems right at the outset.

Another important question is, how long should I look at someone? Well again, you'll want to finish a thought or sentence with one person at a time. That's roughly anywhere between 5-15 seconds. If it's a little longer or shorter that's not a problem.

The main thing is that you look at one person at a time for more than an instant. Of course if you finish an entire paragraph or dissertation with one person it might become suspect. Be natural but don't overdo the amount of continuous eye contact with one individual either.

An additional benefit to Lock, Talk, and Pause, especially with larger audiences, is that when you look at one person in a room filled with hundreds, about 15 people think you're looking at them. Sometimes it's hard to zero in on one pair of eyes, so just pick someone out and focus on them. You may only be focusing on one person as you lock in, but many more are feeling the benefit of your direct eye contact.

Occasionally, when looking around the room, you may sense that the audience is starting to get restless or perhaps they look tired. Maybe it's time to take a break or perhaps it is time to engage your audience.

The Lock, Talk, and Pause Method may feel unusual at first because most of us are not used to looking directly at people for longer periods of time, especially while presenting. After a while, however, like many other things it will become easier.

Once you've got this routine down and it becomes second nature, you'll be ready to energize your message, and you'll wonder how you ever managed without Lock, Talk, and Pause.

Is Looking Good Really That Important?

Cicero once stated, "Without effective delivery, a speech of the highest mental capacity can be held in no esteem while one of the moderate abilities, with this qualification, may surpass even those of the highest talent." Cicero was on to something.

No matter how long you prepare and no matter what your content consists of, you must be able to deliver it effectively. And keep in mind that you never will have a second chance to make a first impression. How you execute this delivery will stay with your audience forever. Whether you want to believe it or not, the fact is people will remember how you looked more than what you said.

Several years ago, psychologist Albert Mehrabian of UCLA conducted a study and did extensive research on presentation skills. Listeners were asked to judge the impact of the communication of speeches. The results were astonishing. How you look (body movement and facial expression) accounted for 55%. Vocal qualities (voice inflection and volume) accounted for 38%. And the words themselves (content) only accounted for 7%.

Impact on Audience

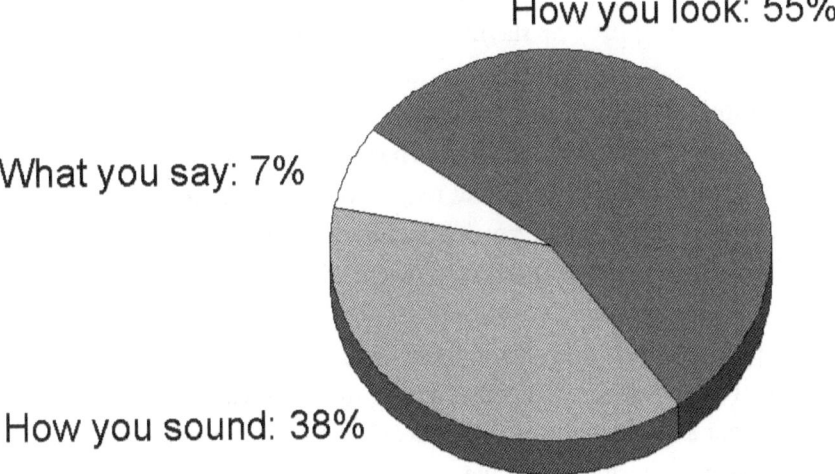

How you look: 55%

What you say: 7%

How you sound: 38%

At first glance, these numbers are amazing, but somehow not surprising. Think about all of the times that you've been to a presentation, meeting, or back to when you were in school. Do you remember the content?

Usually we remember a few lines or perhaps a few details that we think are important, but generally we don't remember a lot of content. It's also difficult for most of us to remember large amounts of content and I don't believe that to be unusual. In fact, many studies confirm that listeners typically remember no more than three separate ideas or concepts per presentation.

We do, however, remember a colorful article of clothing, an interesting visual, or perhaps something funny that happened, like someone tripping on the stage or knocking over a glass of water. Why? Because we saw this come to life right in front of us.

As an amateur anthropologist, I would guess that we relied heavily on our eye sight and vision back in the cave days, watching out for hostile groups, avoiding animals that wanted to eat us, and chasing those we wanted to eat. It was a matter of survival.

Vision and being aware of our surroundings probably took priority over cave etchings, and I would imagine that most cavemen recounted stories about hunting prey or slaying a foe with great visual detail while sitting around the campfire in the evening.

Computer designers and software engineers understand that we remember more what we see than what we hear, or the content. That's why they create desktop icons like recycle bins and briefcases.

That makes sense when you consider that the first etchings on cave walls, (the world's first real desktop) were drawings, not words or hieroglyphics. And when you think about it, people dream in pictures, perhaps moving pictures, but rarely sentences or words.

Typically engineers, physicians, or highly technical individuals tend to be somewhat skeptical about these ideas, and I can appreciate why. I certainly want my physician to have studied a few books and hopefully have remembered some of the content. Hopefully the pilot who will be guiding the next flight I'm on will have done the same.

Is content important? Absolutely! I was raised in an academic home. My father was a college professor who taught Political Science for a state university for almost thirty years. I have an appreciation for content and respect for education.

But when appearing or presenting in public, the rules are different. We're now dealing with performance art. The implementation of proper presentation skills techniques can have dramatic effects, even on the legal system.

Let's consider the famous "trial of the century". Guilty or not guilty, no matter whom you liked or didn't like; who was the one person that everyone remembers from that trial other than O.J. himself? Overwhelmingly, Johnnie Cochran.

Why? Well, he looked good; he used gestures, was dressed sharp, and was extremely animated (55%). He used lots of voice inflection (variance in the pitch or the tone) and had a strong amount of volume when he spoke (38%). Finally whether you liked him or not, he's a very smart guy (7%). He had the whole package.

Did he influence this trial and get a verdict that surprised many who thought O.J. was guilty? Yes! Was he in the background at first and did he then basically take over the courtroom. Yes! Do these presentation skills really work? Absolutely!

Obviously, there might have been other factors that determined the final verdict in the trail and the success of Mr. Cochran. However, no matter what your political or moral beliefs are, you can't argue with what happened and that most people remembered the phrase, "If the glove doesn't fit, you must acquit." Cochran left a rhyming sound bite for everyone to easily remember including the jury, and for me culminated a brilliant display of presentation skills, one of the best orchestrated presentations in memory.

For those of you who still may be skeptical about the power of effective presentation skills, I would like to share a political story with you that clearly, in my opinion, represents the birth of presentation skills, as we know it today.

It was the presidential election of 1960, when Vice-President Nixon was debating John F. Kennedy. A series of debates were scheduled and since TV was still a relatively new medium (there were no color TVs and having a TV at all was considered to be somewhat of a luxury by many) the debates were also broadcast on the radio.

Because of the limited TV viewership back then, many more people got their news information from radio, and this set the stage for an extremely interesting outcome.

The folks who listened to the debate on the radio gave Nixon the thumbs up as far as winning the debate. However, the people watching on TV, overwhelmingly picked Kennedy as the winner. Why?

Nixon was of course always known as an extremely tough campaigner and his no-nonsense attacks on Kennedy and his hard-nosed style seemed to play well as far as content.

On the other side, Kennedy had been out campaigning in California just prior to the debate and had a bronzed tan. JFK looked supremely confident. Also, I think that I wouldn't offend anyone if I said that Kennedy was a better looking, more visually striking figure than Nixon was.

In addition, Nixon appeared nervous and edgy on camera and at one point it even appeared as though he was sweating. Needless to say, Nixon was a mess visually compared to Kennedy, and Kennedy ultimately won the election.

Did image win out over content? Was this the beginning of "look good for the camera"? My thoughts are that it was a pivotal time for presentation skills and media skills. That's when it all really started.

Let's move forward to some other political figures in the more recent past and we can see that "looking good" still seems to impact political success.

In 1980 Ronald Reagan defeated then President Jimmy Carter in the election. Interestingly enough, Carter is considered by historians to be one of the smartest presidents ever to have served this great country. Conversely, Reagan will probably not be judged as the most intelligent.

Why then was Reagan elected for two terms? Why was he also called the "great communicator"?

Well, he was a second rate actor, who perhaps used some acting skills (very similar to presentations skills) to enhance his political power. Regardless of what you may have thought of Reagan, he looked good. He looked presidential. And a second rate actor makes a first rate presenter, and in this case, a two-time President.

Reagan certainly had a pleasant demeanor, and his good-natured tendencies and ever-present smile, without question, served him well. But Reagan knew a lot about the principles of effective communication.

Ex-President Bush tells the story that when he was Vice President; Ronald Reagan kept looking at him during a particular event and noticed that he wouldn't stop peering in his direction.

After a few moments President Reagan came over to him and said, "I've always found it effective to look at a man when I shake his hand." Interestingly enough, eye contact is also an important component of acting.

On trip to Sydney, Australia, I read Mike Shanahan's (two-time Super Bowl winning head coach of The Denver Broncos) best-selling book: *Think Like A Champion*. Mike writes: "Eye contact is very important. Each of the last two times our team visited The White House I noticed that President Clinton looks at you, he never takes his eyes off you, regardless of what's going on. When you're talking to him, you feel as though you are the only other person in the world that exists. He has that unbelievably unique ability to make you feel special."

Shanahan has won two Super Bowls and Clinton was also elected twice to the presidency. The point here is that presentation skills do impact your audience whether you like it or not.

Content, however, is paramount to any presentation. Therefore, know your content and be an expert, but look good when you deliver your message and incorporate effective presentation skills techniques. This will ensure that you have the best of both worlds.

You know your content better than anybody else does; I want to help you get your message across clearly and help you look good in the process. And when all this comes together your integrity and credibility will speak for itself.

As a side note, it's fascinating to me how many in the public eye are just average presenters. Look at the politicians on TV or some of the TV talk show hosts. Some are excellent presenters, but many are marginal at best.

People call me to tell me all of the time! I constantly get reports and updates on how this celebrity looked or how that politician came off. It's rather interesting to observe.

After reading this book you will never look at a presenter whether in person or on TV, the same way again.

Energizing Your Presentation!

Have you ever been to a boring presentation? Most of us have and most of them are boring because there is no life or passion in what the speaker is saying.

In spite of all of the wonderful consultants and public speaking and communication skills companies out there, ineffective presenters are out there and it has reached epidemic proportions.

One petroleum engineer in Bakersfield, California, told me once that he thought it would be perfect if they could only figure out a way to just use audio visual equipment during presentations thereby eliminating live human presenters all together. His point was that human presentations aren't even necessary.

Let's think about this statement? What this individual is basically suggesting is that human contact and human feeling are not important. I disagree.

When you interview someone, would you like to meet that person face to face or maybe just watch a video of him or her? During an election, would you like to read a proposal of what a candidate stands for or would you like to see that person who is running for office actually deliver her message to you in person?

In spite of the Internet and all of the other mediums by which we gain information, the face to face meeting, and human contact will always be significant for our effective communication.

Since people remember more of what they see and hear, as opposed to what they read, it's obvious that we have to add some life to what we present. It can only help us.

So how can we add life to our presentations and wake up the audience?

In a sense, getting nervous before speaking is a good thing, if you know how to properly channel that nervous energy and use it productively to energize your presentation. Think of yourself as a steaming, boiling pot. You have two choices. You can either try to keep the energy inside, or you can unleash it and use it to help vitalize your presentation; essentially, letting the steam out of the pot.

All too often, presenters choose to burn off that nervous energy by fidgeting, holding or grabbing on to things, and walking or rocking back and forth.

I recommend that you learn how to dispense with this energy in a productive way. This will make you feel more comfortable and will help you look better. You'll also start to enjoy giving your presentation, you'll relax, and the audience will feel it.

Let's get specific about some real solutions to help you channel your nervous energy in a useful manner.

Balancing Your Stance

Working from the bottom up. Let's start with your feet and a balanced stance.

Generally, when I do the initial benchmark exercise that I referred to earlier in this book, my classes observe participants rocking back and forth, leaning toward one side, or pacing around the room.

None of these things help your cause. All they do is distract from your message and telegraph to the audience that you're really nervous. That's not the message, I think, that you want to convey.

You don't have to be like Yul Brynner in "The King and I" with your feet way apart, or you don't have to drag in like John Wayne. What I want you to consider is a comfortable balanced stance.

That means hands comfortably down to the sides (neutral position) with feet slightly apart and weight evenly distributed on the balls of the feet. Use your knees like shock absorbers supporting your upper body comfortably. This will help you to avoid favoring one side over the other, and "rocking" back and forth.

Can you take a step forward or back occasionally? Yes, but don't start dancing or rocking (I call this the hula-hoop). Try to stay in one place without appearing like a tree rooted firmly in the ground. This is a typical stance used by actors, athletes, and presenters.

From time to time a woman in the class will ask me if it's O.K. for the ladies to use the beauty pageant stance, meaning one-foot forward and slightly turned. No problem, as long as it looks comfortable, it's not a dis-traction, and it doesn't make you appear nervous.

Pacing back and forth constantly, for no apparent reason, typically drives the audience crazy. Yea, a few overzealous motivational speakers or mid-night TV kitchen appliance hawkers may get away with it, but it gen-erally doesn't fly in the business world.

On the other hand, if you'd like to pause, and take a few steps forward to elaborate on that special point or take a step back to reflect and con-sider something, O.K. But constant non-purposeful movement is weak. It makes you look nervous and unsure, and it looks phony.

Gestures

As I've alluded to, I've worked with thousands of folks in my 10 years of teaching communication skills training and I have seen some really curious things that people do with their hands. I've seen some interesting gestures as well.

Most people really don't know where to put or what to do with their hands. They would just as soon have their arms fall off before a public speaking appearance because they seem to get in the way and accentuate nervousness.

The most favored position for most people's hands is the clasped position. The hands come together like magnets right at the belt buckle point. I say magnets because once those hands come together, there's no way that they're coming apart again. It's as though your hands have been super-glued together. People try to break their hands apart, but it's essentially very difficult to do.

When your hands are together in front of you covering your private parts, it's commonly referred to as the "fig leaf position" (also known as the "hostage position"). Somehow this position always seems a little more popular with the guys.

Then there is of course the "talking fig leaf", where the individual moves their hands while they are together. Needless to say that can be a real distraction, especially when covering your privates.

Occasionally, folks will put their hands clasped together behind their backs, which is commonly referred to as the "reverse fig leaf" or what I like to call "parade rest", for those of you with a military background.

It's also popular to put one or two hands in the pockets. It looks comfortable, but you simply handicap your ability to gesture, describe, and emphasize key points. Audiences after all remember what they see. Don't limit yourself.

Also, having your hands in your pockets typically leads to key swirling or change jingling, and what I term "executive worry beads". People in the audience start to count to themselves silently, "Well, let's see that's about 4 quarters, 3 dimes, and a nickel. I'll bet it's about $1.35."

Obviously, this is distracting and it is hard to describe 'expansion' or a 'big opportunity' to your audience when your hands are in your pants.

Other popular gestures include: The "spider on the mirror" (both hands connected at the fingers moving back and forth). If you can't visualize it, just think of ET touching all of his fingers with a human hand, but then imagine those two hands attached to the same body.

At one point or another we've all seen the "clapper". This person that just keeps clapping their hands together because there's nothing else to do and that's how that individual chooses to let the steam out of the pot.

Then there is the "pointing dancer", a real combo-platter of problems. It's a "Saturday Night Fever" type of movement were the speaker dances and moves back and forth, while pointing up and down. These movements should be reserved for the dance floor.

The Pointing Dancer

Stay away from pointing and using fingers all together. A single finger straight up in the air, no matter which one it is, looks ugly and appears arrogant and condescending. It conjures up images of scolding, road rage, and various cultural insults. Different fingers also mean different things and in a culture as diverse as ours, why take a chance.

Often times people will hold up two fingers and say, "There are three things that I want to tell you about." They see their third finger, but the audience doesn't. It's inconsistent.

Still others will show a complete hand and name five things and count each finger for everything on the list. "The first thing is (grabbing first finger), the second thing is (grabbing second finger)", and so on. It ends up looking like the nursery rhyme about "This little piggy went to the market…" plus it will get your hands together again causing potential magnet problems.

We also tend to play with pens when we present, especially when sitting down. There's nothing more distracting than having a presenter click his pen on and off during a presentation.

The audience is equally distracted by ring turning, finger tapping, lip biting, and hair flipping.

Some other interesting things that occur with the hands are gestures below the belt line. This is what I refer to as "aquatic" gesturing. Unless you're describing a recent occurrence at Sea World or your trip to the aquarium, gesturing below the belt line is meaningless.

One of the most popular positions is the "broken arm" or "Velcro elbow". What happens here is that individuals keep their arm(s) in an apparent invisible sling, and for whatever reason they don't get any air under their arms and as a consequence look like they are stuck in a phone booth.

Break out of the phone booth and take the handcuffs off. You have the whole front of the room with empty space. Use it wisely to mirror visually the story that you are trying to depict, and use your full wing span to describe and explain.

Quite often when one arm is in an apparent sling, the other arm is down at the side, but both hands are clenched fists. This is not very friendly looking or inviting. We need to be more open.

Don't gesture too much. Less is more. You don't want your audience to think that you just went to a presentation skills seminar by over-gesturing.

Some people also use the same gesture over and over again, appearing to be almost like a juggler. If you continue to do this, your gestures become meaningless and convoluted. Continuous, constant motion for no meaningful purpose is not recommended.

So, the point is, figure out exactly what you are going to do with your hands and learn to gesture from the shoulders not the elbows. Use your hands to describe and emphasize. Drop your hands down to your side (neutral position) when you're starting your speech or when you're done gesturing.

For Maximum Impact

- Balance Your Stance

- Use Hands Appropriately

- Increase Volume/Inflection

If you are talking about an increase in sales, show us by raising your arm up. If you mention something about reducing costs, again, show us and make sure that the gesture is different than the one you used for an increase in sales. It's amazing how many presenters will use the exact same gesture for an increase, as they will for a decrease. That's confusing.

When you gesture from the neutral position, your gestures become more emphatic. If everything comes from the middle magnet position it looks like you are stuck in a phone booth again.

Dropping your hands down to your side is of course extremely difficult to do. With most people the hands immediately come back together like magnets or start grabbing things like clothing, various body parts like your face, or they jump back into your pockets.

"White Knuckling", meaning grabbing on to things like podiums or clothing, can have interesting results.

One time in Chicago a man started grabbing his pants during the benchmark exercise and didn't realize why everyone in the room was laughing so hard. Within one minute he had pulled his pair of slacks up so high that they looked like a pair of shorts.

Be careful of what I call time-released gestures. Often times when students are learning these new presentation skills they'll say something, but gesture seconds after the word or group of words that matches the gesture is executed.

The whole thing seems very out of synch for the audience and actually makes for a good laugh. Make sure your gestures are timed to match the words that you are saying. Slowing down can only assist here.

Keep in mind that gesturing helps you think. Have you ever watched someone or noticed someone when they're talking on the telephone. What do they do with the other hand that's not holding the phone? They gesture and they gesture continually. Why? Because it helps them think and it helps them find the right words. Gesturing will help you relax and find the correct dialogue.

Finally, you certainly don't want to appear robotic, but most of us need to think about how we will gesture for whatever concept we're presenting, and how we will bring our emphasis to life with appropriate hand movement.

It takes time and practice, and it needs to be well thought out.

Smiling and an Open Face

Smiling has worked wonders for Ronald Reagan. It's generally a wonderful idea, but of course always use good judgement. Speaking at someone's funeral or introducing a 25% lay-off to employees may not warrant a grin, but generally a happy, smiling, open face is the way to go.

When we look at a newborn for the first time we have an open face. We are loving, we're happy, we're sensitive, we're believable, we're sincere, and we're honest.

Smiling and an Open Face

The best way to create an open face is to raise your eyebrows and smile. Think about looking into that newborns' eyes. It'll make a world of difference when you present and the audience will feel the power of your openness.

People don't care how much you know unless they know how much you care. Sharing a smile and showing your open face will add to your believability.

Voice Inflection and Volume

Sometimes if I'm feeling the need to be humorous, I'll come back from a break in one of my sessions and utter the following words; "It's great to be here ladies and gentleman. I am absolutely thrilled to be here and I've got some exciting words to say about this class. It will undoubtedly be the greatest class that you've ever taken and I can't wait to get started."

The audience starts laughing wildly, because while saying these words which certainly sound inspiring, I use an extremely low-volume, monotone, no-inflection, deadpan delivery. It's a guaranteed laugh, but the point is that the words sound great but it doesn't matter, because my delivery is terrible.

As we all know, most presentations are boring. Most presentations are also delivered in a monotone with very little passion or inflection.

One of the most frequently heard comments from my participants, after returning to the classroom after viewing their own video tape has always been, "I didn't realize how low my voice was or how little inflection that I used". This is typically after I encourage and coach them to, " Double your volume. Shout at us! Scream at us!"

It feels very uncomfortable for most of us to raise our voice in front of a large group, however, doubling or even tripling your volume will not in any way offend anyone or send people home annoyed. I've never heard of someone leaving a speech declaring, "That speaker was just too loud."

When many of us are raised we are told to not speak until we're spoken to or to never speak out of turn. All of these early offerings of guidance are amplified when we are in front of a group to make a presentation.

Even as we enter adulthood and have kids of our own, we still hear the voices of our parents, "Don't raise your voice. Who asked you?" Because of this, it is often times difficult for us to break out, feel relaxed, and truly let go to project our voice.

Always remind yourself to double and even triple your volume, and it will still probably be lower than it should be. If 10 is glaringly loud music, and 1 is virtually inaudible, you need to consistently be at a minimum level of 7, but probably 8 when presenting.

I am often asked about what is the one thing that one can do to take command of a room and establish immediate credibility with an audience. Raising your inflection and volume will grab the audiences' attention instantly. It will also help you to let more steam out of the pot, make you feel more comfortable, and exude higher levels of confidence.

I've done it time and time again as I've delivered speeches literally around the world. It truly works and I know it'll work for you.

Just raising your voice alone, however, is not enough.

One must also incorporate voice inflection, which means variance in the pitch or the tone of the voice. It's simply more interesting to listen to someone who speaks with varying degrees of speed and intonation than to someone who has either a loud barrage of dialogue or a non-stop monotone.

When describing voice inflection it is often times easy to use topography. So for example if someone has very little voice inflection it would be considered to be like the plains of Texas. Some voice inflection might be considered similar to the rolling hills of Santa Barbara (or the foothills), while lots of inflection (where it should be) would be considered to be like The Rocky Mountains.

I once had an Italian in class who told me, "Oh inflection simply means, talking like an Italian?" His point was that inflection comes naturally for Italians. Fair enough.

Where you place your voice inflection and emphasis can also have a profound impact on the meaning of what you say. For example if I say:

"I didn't say he left early."

"I didn't say **he** left early."

"I didn't say he **left early**."

In the previous three identical sentences, the meaning of the sentence changes dramatically depending on which word receives the inflection or emphasis.

As we all know, listening is hard work. Think back at how often you've been tempted to tune-out during a boring presentation, trying desperately to remain awake.

Use variety in your voice. Change the variation in length of the sentences, the loudness, the tone, and the pace. Use different sentence types like assertions, questions, and exclamations.

Variety is the spice of life! Keep your audience interested.

Warming Up Your Voice

As a professional speaker and a former professional singer I must share some tips with you regarding warming up your voice before you present.

Your vocal chords are a muscle like any other muscle in your body. So it's important that you warm up and stretch before any presentation. It is crucial to do especially if you are speaking first thing in the morning.

In the morning if you start out cold and have not warmed up your voice, you'll probably start to squeak. We've all heard someone do that before.

To avoid having it happen to you, try singing in the shower or in your car on the way to your presentation to loosen up your vocal chords.

If you don't like to sing make sure and talk to people before you give your presentation. That's not a bad idea anyhow because it'll make you feel more comfortable with things and it will serve also to warm up your voice.

To further loosen up your vocal chords I recommend drinking warm liquids. These will help while colder liquids will constrict your throat. Warm water, coffee, or tea is fine.

It's also nice to have a glass of water or something to drink close by, just in case you need it. It's embarrassing to have to stop in the middle of a presentation and ask someone to get you something to drink. You never know when you might get a frog in your throat.

Part Three

Content and Organization

Content and The Audience
(It's About Them)

The Greek statesman Pericles once offered, "The man who can think and does not know how to express what he thinks is at a level of him who cannot think."

It amazes me how many speakers still start their speech with a phrase like, "What I have to say isn't really that important", "I know you'd rather be somewhere else right now", "I don't want to take up any more of your time", "I'm really nervous about being up here".

Don't ever apologize for speaking to a group. If you do, you will get off on the wrong foot almost immediately.

Remember that those first impressions last forever and the audience starts to size you up very quickly. Respect the stage, that's what actors do and I call it "The Privilege of the Platform" when it comes to presenting. Individuals have taken their time to listen to you and they could probably be doing other things, so respect them and chances are they will respect you.

Everything that we've done up to this point is to take charge of the audience and to get their attention.

In my classes I use exercises initially where people talk about things that are familiar to them (ex: vacations, funny stories, anecdotes) when we practice physical skills. The reason is that I don't want them to worry about content yet. I want them to focus on changing physical behavior in front of complete strangers, and that's hard to do.

But now that we've mastered the physical skills, we've got to focus on content. Looking good is the first step, but at this point we have to have something meaningful to say.

Ethel Merman once said, "I know my lines; what's there to be nervous about?" That's an extremely important point. The great-unsolved mystery of public speaking for me will always be, "You know the content, they don't, why are you nervous?"

Before we even begin to think about the content we must first examine the audience; it's what I term an audience analysis. Your audience for your presentation is without question the most important variable affecting your content, yet ironically, it's one of the most overlooked areas of public speaking.

For example, have you ever been to a presentation where everyone already knew what the speaker was talking about? Or have you been to a presentation where the speaker was speaking over everyone's head?

Surprisingly, it happens more often than not. Just think back to the last two or three presentations that you've been to.

What's critical here is that you connect with your audience. You know how it feels when the presenter has not done their homework and taken the time to get to know you. Don't make the same mistake.

It's crucial for all presenters to engage in a thorough audience analysis before even thinking about structure or content.

Here are some of the important things for you to consider before developing the content of your presentation:

Who will be in the audience? Subordinates, management, well-wishers, or naysayers?

Is this presentation intended to be motivational, informational, or other?

Why should your audience listen to what you have to say?

What makes your speech relevant to them?

What do you have in common with them?

What is the audience's attitude towards your subject matter?

How knowledgeable is the audience about the subject matter you will be delivering?

Will some, all, or no one know who you are?

Are they there because they want to be there or because they have to be there?

How will you be introduced?

What expectations might they have?

What have they been told about you?

What is their profession or occupation?

What's their level of experience and education?

How many people will attend?

How long will the presentation be?

Will there be time for questions?

Will you take questions, answer questions, or get back to them on questions?

What are some of the toughest questions you might expect?

What time of day will you be presenting?

How many others will have spoken before you, and what will they speak about?

Are you planning on using handouts or leaving information or business cards?

How will the audience view you, 'one of us', 'outsider', etc.?

Is there anything you can say or do to relate to them?

How much can you find out about them ahead of time?

Not to be presumptuous, but I'm sure many of you are thinking, "Gee, I hadn't thought of that."

Keep in mind that this is certainly not to be considered the ultimate complete definitive list. There are an endless amount of questions we could add here, but I think this is a good start.

Focus on, "What's important to them? What's going to get their attention?" Remember it's about **them**, not you.

Organization

Before organizing your presentation keep reminding yourself that less is more. Also consider that most presentations have far too many details.

You should be able to put the gist of your presentation into one sentence or what I like to call a headline. What would the headline of your speech be? Think about it. If you can't put that into one sentence you may have to simplify your idea.

It's also probable that you're idea has never been heard by your audience before. In other words, it may be old news to you, but very likely something new to your audience. If you're on a traveling road show giving the speech over and over again, no matter where you go on the whistle-stop tour, it's always their first time. Don't forget that.

Most presentations end up having too much content, although ironically presenters always fear not having enough to say.

Most presenters end up using the "kitchen sink" approach and tell their audiences all they can, about everything they can, in the short amount of time allocated to them. Therefore it becomes a race to spew out as much information as possible as quickly as possible, essentially a self-serving data dump. How disheartening for the audience.

Your presentation is about your audience, not about you finishing everything you want to say as quickly as possible.

Although we'd like to believe it, nobody can recall everything that you say anyway. So choose to make your headline important, relevant to your audience, and to the point.

The old school rule of thumb has always been; tell 'em what you're gonna' tell 'em, tell 'em, and then tell 'em what you told 'em. This model is simple, there's a common thread here, and in this representation the message does not become convoluted.

Let's develop this model for our purposes.

The Organizational Outline

There are many templates or guidelines for organizing presentations. I've put together more or less "The Greatest Hits" compilation of organizational templates with special recommendations for opening and closing.

This outline is medium sized relative to the different formats out there and can certainly be shortened or lengthened depending upon the type of presentation you are making. Here is the basic outline:

Start with a "Grabber"
Problem/Opportunity
Solution/Recommendation
Support With Evidence
Benefits To Audience
Call To Action/Next Steps
End with a "Bang"

The "Grabber"

Why not arouse the audiences' curiosity with a shocking fact, a thought-provoking question, or anything that immediately engages them? That's what I call a "grabber".

Many believe that the structure of a speech should be similar to reading a novel where you slowly build the plot and then the climax occurs. Big mistake!

Remember that the audience is sizing you up in the first thirty seconds and they are thinking about, "Does this person know what they're talking about? Am I going to listen? What's in it for me?" Use that first sentence, those first few words to make a major impact on your audience and take command of the room.

We've all heard the teasers or "grabbers", as I like to call them, that TV stations throw out there to get your attention to make sure that you watch the next show or that you watch the upcoming news.

Local affiliate news stations are notorious for doing this especially during sweeps or ratings week. They'll mention something during a commercial break during the show before the 11 o'clock news to make sure that you tune in.

They entice you with something like, "Coming up at eleven, exercise can actually be bad for you. Tune in tonight to find out more." One of my favorites, "A common food that we all eat reported contaminated". Notice they don't mention what type of food.

If you don't believe this stuff, just watch the show before the news. Stations do this all the time and they also do it during their newscast as they head out to a commercial break. "When we come back, two Kindergartners run off to Vegas to get married. You won't want to miss this." It seems as though we get tricked into watching stuff.

Funny how the story is never quite that crazy once you finally see it, since many times the writers have stretched a little to get you to watch. But the point is, it works! We end up tuning into these news reports that end up being somewhat different than we expect, but these stations are masterful at getting us to take just one more look.

I'm certainly not suggesting that you incorporate dishonesty to get people to listen, but you should whet the audience's appetite so they won't tune out. It's what I call using a "grabber".

For example if someone wants to make a presentation on e-business, he might open with, "Did you know that in just ten years, over half of all products bought in the world will be purchased through the Internet?" Of course we'd want to quote a reputable source on these figures etc.

When speaking about customer service you might say, "You know when I checked into my hotel during my last visit to Seattle, I asked someone at the front desk when breakfast would start and they told me that it's not their job to know that". Again we get attention.

In my public speaking classes my "grabber" changes from time to time depending on the audience, but the universal one that I can always rely on is, "Did you know that public speaking is the number one fear that people have, according to a lot of studies?"

With a larger audience, another version of that might be me raising my hand and asking, "How many of you get nervous when you think of making a public presentation". Quite a few will raise their hand, especially if there are several hundred people in the audience. Then I respond with, "Notice, my hand is up too." A little self-deprecation adds a nice touch.

Sometimes I use, "Did you know that people are twice as afraid of speaking in public as they are of dying? That's amazing when you think about it." That's an interesting version to throw out there because people are invariably astonished by this fact. It also let's everyone immediately know that public speaking is at the top of the list of fears that people have.

Grabbing the audiences' attention is not as difficult as you may think, yet I am not suggesting that you scramble for some bogus dramatics or make up erroneous information at the cost of losing credibility. But if you have the time, and you ask others in your industry, you will find a "grabber" that's appropriate.

Many times in my sessions, someone will indicate that they can't think of a "grabber". Invariably we have a class discussion about it, we all ask a few questions, and I have yet to have a participant not come up with an audience-grabbing opening statement; although some are certainly more thought out and better than others.

Take extra time and care with developing your "grabber", it's your first impression it's worth being well composed. The "grabber", incidentally, is the perfect lead into the problem or the opportunity.

Sometimes presenting a problem connected to the consequences of no action can be powerful as well. For example, "If we don't stop the hackers from breaking into our web site, we could all be out of business."

On the other hand, if you can present an opportunity you may be able to connect some type of reward to the success of your idea. "If we can

expand our global markets by 25% over the next 2 years, our profit sharing could double, even triple". Now you've got the audiences' attention,
and that's a great way to start.

Problem/Opportunity

The "grabber" introduces the problem/opportunity. Make sure that
the problem/opportunity is one that everyone can relate to and that it is
expressed in a way that everyone can understand. And the more familiar you are with this situation, the more likely your presentation will
sound credible.

Think in terms of headlines when developing your problem/opportunity.
What would the headline of your speech be? Don't get too verbose or wordy
when considering your opening problem/opportunity. An information data
dump will serve to confuse your audience and make your credibility come
into question.

Your headline might be "Opening up our business to e-commerce will
help us grow, not shut us down." That's one main idea and it's clear.

Solution/Recommendation

Next, you'll want to present your solution or recommendation. Most of
us don't have a problem doing this, but the key is held in the language that
you use in presenting it.

Never be arrogant or talk down to your audience as in, "you will" or
"you must". People like to be romanced. Even if they know something is
good for them, let them discover it for themselves. Seduce us, don't
threaten us. Use words like, "Please consider this." Or "Here's an idea that
I'd like you to think about".

Naturally there are times in business where you must take more of a hard line direct approach, but generally I've found that people like to come to conclusions on their own.

Make absolutely sure that you are very comfortable with the details of your solution/recommendation. It's at the heart of what you are presenting and if you are not well versed with what you're proposing, it could spell big trouble for you.

Be confident and enthusiastic about your recommendation. This is the main event.

You've set it up nicely with your "grabber" and presented it as a problem/opportunity. Here's your chance to share your wonderful idea. Revel in it!

Support with Evidence

You'll want to support that great solution/recommendation of yours with evidence. Your audience, just like you wants to see proof. For many of us, "seeing is believing."

There are four basic different types of evidence: personal, statistics, example, and analogy. Consider your audience to help you to decide which type of evidence to choose.

Typically you'll need a minimum of one piece of evidence (unless your talk is purely informational) to support your idea and rarely more than two pieces of evidence. It also depends on the length of your talk.

I would normally suggest that you take your strongest piece of evidence and run with that. Keep it simple and don't oversell the audience. Of course there are always exceptions to the rule and if you have some extra convincing to do, by all means load the deck with more proof.

The first type of evidence is personal. Perhaps you were there or you saw something happen. This is probably the most interesting and powerful form of evidence. It also gives you extra credibility with your audience.

I've heard many speeches in my life and it seems that the most captivating are relative to someone talking about what happened to them personally.

If a safety expert comes on and speaks about the statistics of airline safety, that's interesting, but imagine talking to an actual plane crash survivor. Which holds more interest?

The same goes for someone talking about a disease. Would you rather hear about statistics or would you rather talk to someone who has been personally affected by a disease or has overcome a serious illness?

One night, I was having dinner with executives of a pharmaceutical company for whom I had delivered a workshop earlier that day and we all started talking about gun control.

The table was fairly split on this hotly contested subject. About half wanted tighter gun control and the other half was for the Second Amendment and the right to bear arms, etc. Naturally, both sides were quoting statistics and supporting their respective points of view, when something very interesting happened.

One of the executives who was in favor of gun ownership told a story about how he was in college and had worked at a liquor store part time to support himself. He went on to explain that late one night a man came in and held him up at gunpoint and actually shot him, even though he had turned over all the money in the cash register.

Fortunately this man, now a pharmaceutical executive, was not fatally injured, but he still carries fragments of the bullet that entered his body right next to his spinal chord.

He lives a normal life, however, his comment was interesting, "I wish I would have had a gun to shoot back and defend myself. I'm definitely for the right to bear arms!" Everyone at the table was stunned.

No matter what side of the argument we had come down on, it made everyone stop and consider a side we normally wouldn't have had we just heard more statistics. Statistics are used abundantly by pharmaceutical companies, but this group was most affected by the personal remembrance of one of their own.

Using statistical evidence or numerical facts arranged for analysis and interpretation are great for technical people and financial people. They can also simplify large quantities of information for people that aren't technically oriented.

Statistics may also point out some real surprises or interesting findings that get the audience's attention. It is a desirable form of evidence to present, and is generally considered to be very effective in the business world.

However, don't fall in the trap of presenting too many statistics or numbers at once. You will serve to lose and confuse the audience. You may also jeopardize your own believability, if you yourself don't fully understand the statistics being presented. I've seen it happen many times. Remember to keep it simple, be clear, and be concise so we can all relish in the wisdom of your easy to understand message.

Another effective use of evidence in business would be examples. That's what I've been doing throughout this book when I share stories about what works and what doesn't.

By giving people examples it's easier for them to grasp and think, "Yes, this could work here too." It facilitates an openness to attempt something if it has worked before.

If it's an example from a similar industry or even a different department in your company, and the example seems "close to home"; it makes it so much easier to sell your idea. Try to make your example as tightly parallel to your own solution or recommendation as possible. It could make your idea a "slam dunk".

On the other hand, an analogy can serve to paint the big picture of understanding. It also makes a case for creating great visuals to mirror your thoughts. The tip-of-the-iceberg analogy is one of the most common used in business to warn against an impending larger doom that lurks just below the surface.

The right analogy can make a lasting impression with listeners and the image of that iceberg or forest through the trees will hopefully be something that is burned into the hard drive of your audience.

Benefits to the Audience

When I was in high school, I started writing articles for the school newspaper my freshman year and ended up being sports editor before too long.

To save up a few extra dollars for college and gain journalistic practice, I worked for a local newspaper in Orange County, California, called "The Placentia News-Times". I would write stories about school occurrences and cover local happenings.

Leland Pound, the editor of The Placentia News-Times, always told me back then, "Till, make sure and include the people's names. The more names the better. Also, let's get pictures of these people and print them in the paper." Invariably we'd send out a photographer who'd snap some pictures.

The lesson I learned from Mr. Pound was that people like to see their name and their picture in print. It sells newspapers, especially if it's a small local paper. This all reminds me of the mentality many have about elections.

It's been said that most people are apathetic about voting. Barely fifty percent of eligible voters cast their ballot in presidential elections. However, recently when there has been a proposal in my local community to convert a closed military base into an international airport, you wouldn't believe the local reaction and involvement. I've never seen so many politically active people in my life.

But what's the point and what's the lesson here? Simply stated, "If it's about me or my vital interests, I'm interested. If not, I don't really care that much."

Imagine if your community were considering a ballot measure to put a maximum-security prison in a place where a beautiful park used to be. Do you think that might get a few people off the couch who normally wouldn't consider it?

This basic principal of human nature is important to understand when thinking about any part of your presentation. It's especially important in reconnecting your audience with the benefits to them.

So we've supported our idea with evidence. What we need now is to tie that evidence back to the needs of the audience. Always ask yourself, "What does all of this mean to the audience?" It's is crucial.

Make sure that your audience is aware of the great importance of your point to them. For example, "What this means to you is greater earnings in the future"…"more opportunities for growth within the organization"…"job security". Whatever that positive connection to the audience is, make it very clear.

In my business, trainers often talk about everyone's favorite radio station being WIIFM, "What's In It For Me?" Keep it tuned to whatever station your audience is listening to and your ratings will go through the roof.

Call to Action/Next Steps

Now we have to mention to the audience what the next steps or the call to action is.

You've gotten them motivated. You've excited them. You've done it all with great style and panache. What do you want them to do? Don't forget to finish your job by asking them to do some things for you by being as specific as possible.

I just love when presenters end speeches like this, "Thanks for your support"…"I appreciate your time, let's stay in touch"…"Please do what you can".

That's not good enough, and you'll just end up shortchanging yourself. Be very precise in what you expect and don't leave anything to chance.

"I need everyone to write their congressman" (and have that address in a handout or up on the screen). Or, "At the end of the month we'll be meeting again, so please e-mail your suggestions to me by the 15th. I need at least two paragraphs from everyone." That beats the heck out of, "Please, get back to me with your thoughts".

Or perhaps you need to mention what criteria must be met, who specifically will be responsible for what, and how this all will be measured.

Either way, make sure that your message is on the top of the in-basket and not at the bottom of the circular file. Be precise and ask for specifics.

Ending with A "Bang"

Your last words should leave your audience inspired or with something to think about.

Maybe you'll want to go back to the idea of your "grabber". Perhaps you'll want to remind them one more time on how your idea impacts them. Maybe you'll want to encapsulate the key points of your speech.

Whatever you do, end it on a positive high note and conclude with confidence. Your audience will especially remember the beginning and the end.

We may not all be as eloquent as Winston Churchill, but he certainly set a glorious example for closing a speech that grips your heart and elevates your spirit.

In 1940 in a speech to the House of Commons, Churchill ended with, "Let us...brace ourselves to our duties, and so bear ourselves that if the British Empire and its Commonwealth last for a thousand years, men will still say, 'This was their finest hour'."

I've heard many speakers conclude their speeches by declaring that the definition of insanity is doing the same thing year after year, but expecting different results. It's an interesting way to end a speech because it is a "call to action", an ending with a "bang", and a wake-up call, all rolled into one.

Finally, when doing these presentations always remember who the audience is. Try not to use inside lingo that only a few people understand.

If you use acronyms make sure everyone knows what they mean, for example, "There are not as many pre-IPOs, that would be pre-Initial Public Offering stock offerings made available to regular investors like you and I, but that's beginning to change."

No one will fault you for explaining an acronym or insider lingo, but someone will miss your point if you don't explain it to everyone or assume that everyone knows.

How Long Should Your Presentation Be?

Most experts, myself included, agree that a presentation should generally last no longer than 20 minutes. After 20 minutes people typically start tuning out. People's attention span is not that long and my belief is that TV has had a tremendous influence on all of this.

Ronald Reagan, who understood the medium of television as well as anybody, believed that any speech over 20 minutes was too long. Interestingly enough, The Gettysburg Address was only about 3 ½ minutes long.

A TV show rarely goes longer than 15 minutes without a commercial. Segments on news magazine shows like 60 Minutes, 20/20, and Dateline typically run 15-18 minutes. Yes, TV has trained all of us to pay attention for only short periods of time. That's just the way it is.

Today we live in a world of sound bites and this all started changing back in the early 70's when 35-40 second segments of a politician giving a speech were transformed into 10-15 seconds on television.

It's changed so dramatically, that it is now common to see network anchors talk about a politician as you see that politician's image behind the anchor on a big screen, while the anchorperson paraphrases and reduces an entire speech to one sound bite.

The networks started to realize the potential revenue from their news shows and media consultants explained to network executives that people prefer action sequences, crime chases, catastrophe and disaster footage, etc.

What the TV viewers don't want to see is another talking head. That's why on average network anchors Brokaw, Jennings, and Rather, are only on camera between 5 to 6 minutes during a newscast, that's it.

I can remember when I was a kid they used to show the marching band on TV during the halftime show of football games. Well, guess what? They don't anymore. They go to "live" remotes with other players, highlights and recaps of other games, anything but showing the marching band.

So to be successful and memorable, your presentations need to be high energy, entertaining, not too long, and to the point.

Transitions

Marlon Perkins of "Mutual of Omaha's Wild Kingdom" had some of the weirdest transitions that I can still remember to this day. He'd say things like, "Well just like leopards have spots, you too need life insurance."

Obviously this is not a good transition, so make sure that there is a logical, legitimate connection between things.

Transitions are wonderful and some people are better at it than others. If the transition seems logical, fine. Go for it. But don't force yourself to make transitions that seem awkward. Silence is better than a forced transition.

You also don't need to transition on every point. Sometimes less is more and avoiding a transition occasionally may serve to keep listeners on the edge of their seats.

Vary your transitions and avoid using the same group of words again and again. "That leads me to my next point…" "That leads me to my next point…" "That leads me to my next point…"

Some effective transitions might be: "That is why I'm recommending we...." "Remember when I talked about..." "You've all probably been wondering, why should we do this?" "What does all of this mean to you?" "Why do I think this is going to work?"

Are You In The Know, and Do You Know Where You Are?

If you're a road warrior like me, sometimes you forget where you are. For that reason it's important to remind yourself, "Hey, I'm in the Northwest" or "I'm in Big Sky Country-Montana". The audience will sense if you don't really care about where you are.

Take pride in knowing something about the area where you are presenting. Don't overdo it, but just make a statement to let them know, "This is my first trip to Montana and now I know why they call it 'Big Sky Country'".

When in South Dakota I mentioned that I spent the previous afternoon checking out Mt. Rushmore. My audience knew that I knew where I was. That's the point.

On that same note, weave in current events into your presentation. Perhaps you need to do it only once, but it let's them know that you're on top of things and that you're not stale. Even a mention that the market closed way up or way down the day before will indicate that you're up to speed.

Sporting events can let people know immediately that you're not completely out of touch or not interested in their community. Perhaps you know how the local team is doing.

There's always something going on whether it be basketball or football playoffs, or the baseball pennant race. Huge sporting spectacles like The Indy 500, The Kentucky Derby, The Masters, The World Series, The

Super Bowl, The Stanley Cup, and March Madness can be the topic of conversation and somehow incorporated into your speech.

Popular movies (that haven't been released on video yet), hit songs, or popular musical groups or artists let people know that you're hip.

If you have no idea how to show that you're "in the know", just pick up the local or national paper that's probably been delivered to your hotel room door, and read it as you drink the coffee from the coffee maker in your room.

Whatever you decide to talk about to let them know that you "know what's going on", you'll get extra points if you can relate it directly to your speech. For example, "Well, just like those Cowboys, I feel like a real winner today, to be talking to all of you!" Or you could say, "Well the market's way down, but I know your company is doing exceptionally well with the introduction of the new..."

Comments like these show respect to your listenership and will make it easier for you to win them over.

Humor and Jokes

It's amazing to me how many professional speech coaches still insist that their clients use humor right up front to warm up the audience.

Personally, I love humor. I love to laugh! I feel that people don't laugh enough as it is and take themselves way too seriously.

When I was a freshman in college I actually thought about being a standup comic. After a few stints at the Comedy Store in LA, I realized how incredibly difficult it was to be consistently funny.

I also realized how highly intelligent and talented the most successful comics like Jay Leno (who I met on several occasions back then) and David Letterman really are. It gave me a profound respect for professional comedians and comedy.

Telling a joke or using humor is very risky business! First off, most people if asked would suggest that you use humor at the beginning of a presentation to "loosen up" the crowd. Big high risk gamble!

You are at your highest state of fear, the audience is sizing you up, and you're going to roll the dice with humor. Unless you're extremely confident about what you're doing and you know your audience very well, don't take a chance with humor. Why?

To begin with, many of us aren't that funny. Even if we have a joke professionally written for us not everyone is able to pull it off.

Being a comedian is very hard work. Ask any comedian out there. They'll all tell you about the night that they "bombed" and that's what these guys do for a living. Being funny is simply harder than it looks.

Some audiences may view humor as not taking them and their business seriously enough. Therefore, you are better off feeling the audience out first and then easing your way into some humor as you get more comfortable and if it feels right.

If your presentation is going well and your audience appears to be receptive, don't force humor either. Stay with what is working for you.

The other real dilemma with humor is; what can you really talk about in today's politically correct times? Sex, politics, race, religion? All the fun stuff is off limits for obvious reasons.

All it takes is one little remark that offends one person and your career could be seriously damaged. When I speak of people's sensitivity and that it only takes one time or one person, I learned that from personal experience.

I can't reveal exactly what I said, but I will admit that, years ago I made an extremely mild reference to a subject relating to sex and gender. Even if I were to write out the details in this book, probably 99.9% of you would absolutely not be offended, but that's not the point. One person took offense and it did get back to me and I had some explaining to do later.

Keep in mind that I'm known to be fairly diplomatic and easy going by nature, but I learned that it wasn't worth it to joke about anything that could possibly offend someone.

Take it from me. I made a mistake and I hope that my mistake can be a lesson for everyone else.

Fortunately, this situation did not cause me great difficulty, but it was a great wake-up call nevertheless. I'll never forget it.

Self-deprecating humor is the easiest and safest type of humor. Make fun of yourself; people love that. But resist making fun of others, because it's generally just not a good idea.

Often times in my seminars I'll discuss my terrible handwriting, or my lack of ability to draw, etc. I'm making fun of myself and I haven't offended anyone else. That's playing it safe.

If you decide to use humor and I hope that you use it successfully, that doesn't mean that your speech is not important. Whenever you get up in front of a group make sure that you have something important to say, even if you are on a serious comedic roll. Don't get drunk with the success of a few laughs and wander astray. Stay focused.

In case you tell a joke that bombs, the best comebacks that I've heard are: 1) "Some jokes I do just for me." 2) "I would now like you to bow your heads and join with me in silent prayer for that last joke that just died." 3) "That is the last time I buy a joke from (key member of the organization)."

Finally, keep your eye on the ball and remember what others have said before you, especially if there's a long row of speakers. I once heard some-one tell a joke during a presentation that had been told just minutes ear-lier by the previous speaker. That's not funny.

Part Four

Visuals

Designing Visuals

Before we address dealing with visuals mechanically we need to talk about design.

Most visuals used in business are bullet point visuals. Charts and graphs follow in popularity, and finally we see pictures. Actually we have it backwards. People get bored with bullet point visuals or words because that's what they see all the time.

Of course, speakers love them because they've got their cheat sheet right there in front of them. But remember it's about your audience. Audiences love pictures, but it's the type of visual you really see least of. Graphs and charts are somewhere in the middle as far as actual usage and prevalence.

We can't always use pictures effectively, but just like thinking of analogies or "grabbers" it can be done. Can the "tip of the iceberg" conjure up an image? Sharks swimming around your sinking ship may indicate what...?

I'm not asking you to pick up where Charles Schulz, of "Peanuts" fame left off, but I am suggesting that you break up the monotony of 50 bullet point visuals in a row. It's too boring and we've all seen it before.

We also discussed at the very beginning of this book how important pictures are in terms of what the audience actually remembers. They will remember images more than words.

Statistical information is also more easily presented with charts or graphs versus huge spreadsheets with small non-legible numbers. It's easier to grasp for the audience and it's easier for you to explain.

Designing Visuals Effectively

Before

After

Sales by Region

Sales by Region	
South	$395,000
West	$740,000
North	$164,000
East	$350,000
Total	$1,649,000

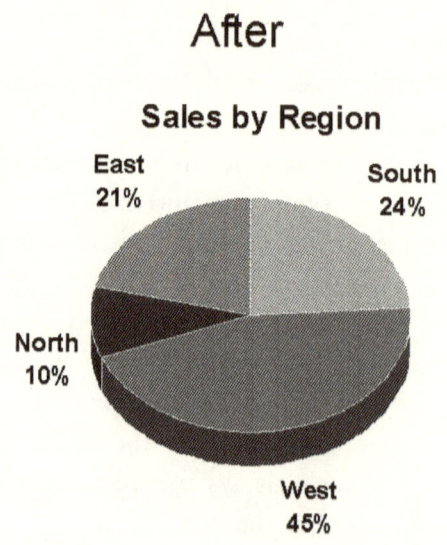

Sales by Region

The basic ground rules for designing visuals are fairly logical but are generally disregarded. Let's review some of the basics.

First, remember the rule of KISS (Keep It Super Simple or if you prefer Keep It Simple Sweetheart).

It's amazing how many presenters are confused by their own visuals. How often have you seen a presenter say, "Well, ah, here, you see, um well, what I think this is ah, well I believe this, um well…"

It's hard to believe that a presenter would even consider using a visual that he or she doesn't understand. What a rude statement to the audience; "Your time is so unimportant to me that I haven't even taken the time to understand my own visual."

Make it easy on yourself and others. There is no need for an unsolved mystery here or for you to become a prisoner of your own poorly designed visual.

If it's a really complicated concept, give us a basic overview with a visual and break it down in subsequent visuals. Or, you may leave us a handout to take home, so that we may further study the complexity of what it is you're trying to convey.

In keeping with KISS, make sure that you don't have more than one concept per visual and consider that less is more. Naturally, there are always exceptions to the rule.

If you must create a more complex visual because you're an engineer or physician, give us an overview slide, so we can see the "big picture". After that you can get more in depth, if it's absolutely necessary.

Obviously, you'll still use bullet point visuals from time to time, and there are some general guidelines here as well. Many consultants advocate the 4x4, 5x5, or 6x6 method, which basically means no more than four, five, or six bullets per visual, and no more than four, five, or six words per bullet.

That's generally not a bad rule of thumb because it forces the designer of the visual not to jam too many words on one page. Besides, if there are too many words on a visual the temptation is always to start reading.

If you're putting enough words on the visual to violate the 6x6 parameter, then it's either a script or generally too much information for just one visual anyhow.

On occasion, it's necessary for a CEO or someone in business to read a quote that might be a paragraph or two. That's fine. As long as it's the exception and not the rule.

In a case like this, you may want to move slightly to your right and step up towards the audience and then look at the screen, so you can read it. Before a quote or passage does appear on the screen, you can introduce it in the following way, "I'd like to share with you our mission statement. Please feel free to follow along as I read this to you."

This let's your audience know what's coming. They will follow along as you read it to them, and they'll probably finish reading it long before you do. That's why I recommend this to be the exception.

When designing visuals, be colorful (not just black and white), and use more pictures, charts, and graphs than words if possible. The audience will love you for it, and they will remember more.

It is also important to understand that western audiences read from top to bottom and left to right. This is how they will process the information whether you like it or not, and should very clearly indicate how you will layout your visual.

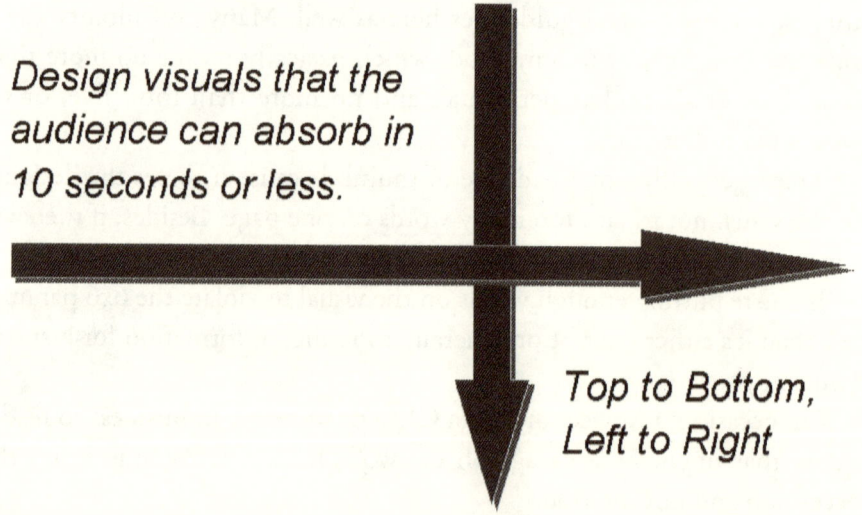

First they'll look at the top of any visual. That's natural because that's how we read in this culture. For this reason, don't put a heading at the bottom or your visual, unless that's the last thing you want your audience to see.

If you're using overheads, design your visuals horizontally. Been to the movies lately? Take a long look at the screen. Design your visuals in the landscape style because people read from left to right and our eyes are in our head horizontally not vertically.

Delivery with Visuals

Dealing with visuals in front of an audience is again a fairly logical process, however, surprisingly few presenters manage their visuals effectively.

The first problem with visuals is that they are a distraction for the audience. In other words, when you present a visual to the audience for the first time they will look at it, because they are curious.

Unfortunately this distracts from the presenter and momentarily makes the speaker seem almost invisible. Again, the presenter essentially vaporizes because the audience has never seen the visual before and they will study it until they've figured out what the visual represents.

At this point you have two choices. You can either verbally go through the visual as the audience is processing it, or you can talk about something else. If you choose to talk about something else, they won't hear a word you say.

The common mistake is for presenters to mention their transition or some type of introductory phrase at this juncture, but as soon as the visual is up on the screen no one will hear the transition or introduction. They're looking at the visual!

If you want to set up a slide with an introduction or transition, that's fine, but do so before you show your visual. Don't fight the natural flow of information as so many speakers do.

Once your visual has been displayed, you should verbalize its message in simple terms from top to bottom and left to right, just as the audience is processing it.

Do you have to use the exact words of the visual? No, but I strongly suggest that you stay pretty close to what's up there on the screen, otherwise you're talking apples and they're thinking oranges. That's not good communication.

You can see why KISS and the design of visuals are so important. It all starts to fall into place, logically. Don't fight the audience's natural instincts, you're facilitating. Describe the visual to them, as they will process it. There's simply no reason to try to swim upstream or do anything else.

Absorb, Align, and Address

How do you physically handle visuals and how do you deal with them mechanically?

Ideally, position yourself to the right of the screen as you face the audience (the audience's left as they face the screen), because they read from left to right and then will see you before the visual.

If you're forced to be away from the screen off to the side or at a podium, that's fine, but again may I advise you to stand to the right of the screen as you face the audience if you have the choice, and typically you will.

You'll want to maintain a nice balanced stance and do what I call Absorb, Align, and Address. Let me elaborate.

First, from wherever you are standing, you'll want to look at the top of the screen in silence. NEVER TALK TO THE SCREEN! Only talk to the audience.

Never Talk To The Screen

- **Absorb**
(in silence)

- **Align**
(with eyes)

- **Address**
(the audience)

You'll also want to make sure that you are facing the audience with your shoulder blades parallel to the screen or back wall. That way you're not turning your back on the audience or one side of the room.

Many times when presenters start to look at a screen behind them, they start to slowly turn their bodies in the process. After several slides the natural progression is for one half of the audience to only see the backside of the presenter.

This is not professional and shows disrespect to those only seeing your back. Make sure that the entire front of your body always faces the audience.

Looking at the screen in silence is called the Absorb step. Your are essentially absorbing and thinking about what you are going to tell the audience while you study your visual.

Absorb in silence for as long as you need to. Some, like myself occasionally like to put the left hand up (as a virtual pointer) to guide through the visual and that's fine if you like it, but it's not necessary.

Sometimes using your left hand as a pointer becomes repetitive and mechanical. In addition, many times the screen isn't close enough to you to be able to touch anyhow, although your hand can still be a guide from afar.

Once you've absorbed the first bullet point, concept or idea, Align with one pair of eyes and Address (speak to) that audience member using an appropriate gesture with your right hand, if it happens to fit.

I don't know if this will assist you, but one of my students referred to this whole process as "Twist and Shout". It may help you remember, but of course you don't want to be continuously twisting and turning, because that will only distract.

Then you look at the next bullet point, concept, or idea and go through the same process again. Absorb, Align, and Address.

Once the visual has been covered, you can step away from the screen or the wall and come up to the audience and elaborate on the visual. Since the visual is still behind you, you can always pause and look back silently at a certain point on the screen to get your bearings.

In my experience, so many people forget this important point. It's O.K. to look back at the screen in silence, BUT resist the temptation of talking to the screen. Make eye contact (Align) with the audience before you start to speak.

Once you've addressed the meaning of the visual, you can elaborate on each point as often and in whichever order you would like. If you've removed the curiosity factor of the visual for the audience, their eyes will be focused back on you. Always remember to neutralize the curiosity first so that you don't erase your own image.

It should take about ten seconds or less to verbally neutralize the attraction of the visual for the audience. That's a basic guideline. If it goes a little longer or a little shorter, that's fine. If they're still wondering, "What does this thing up there mean?" 30 seconds after it has been unveiled, you probably haven't explained it correctly, or your visual is too confusing.

To be clear, the position next to the screen is the "remove the curiosity" position and the second position out towards the audience is the "elaboration" position.

Position Yourself

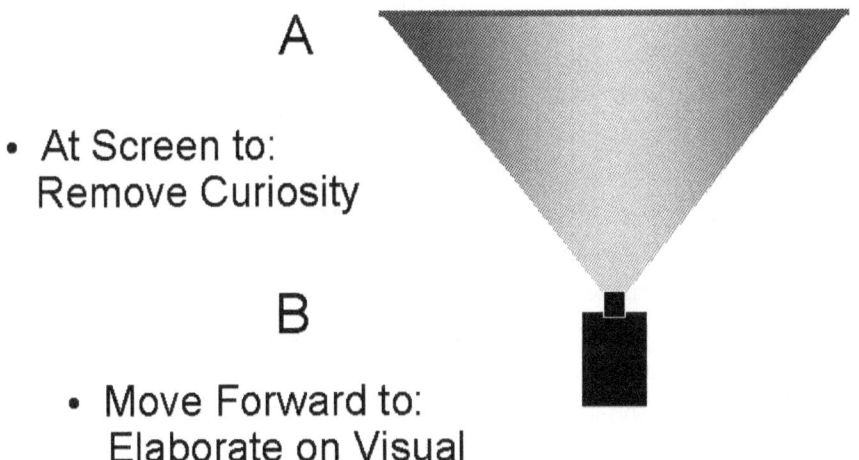

A

- **At Screen to:
Remove Curiosity**

B

- **Move Forward to:
Elaborate on Visual**

Many of my students get stuck up at the screen. It's O.K. to come out and talk to us once you've removed the curiosity of that visual using the Absorb, Align, and Address method.

That's also why you don't have to use your left hand as a virtual pointer all the time, while up at the screen. It's certainly effective to do so, but if you force yourself to do it all of the time for each visual, sometimes you can feel "stuck" next to the screen.

One of the great dangers of the audiovisual equipment like overhead, slide, or laptop projectors is that these items attract presenters like a magnet.

When you move from the screen back to the front of the room, don't start fiddling with or leaning on the equipment or playing with things on the table it's on. Stay away from the equipment, so you won't distract the audience.

Often times, people ask me about the funniest thing I've ever seen during a presentation.

This question always reminds me of a pharmaceutical group I worked with in Portland, Oregon, years ago and clearly indicates how befuddled people can get during a presentation. Back then we were using overhead projectors exclusively and the class would create visuals using colored markers and transparencies.

Each time one lady in this particular class went up to present and attempt to move to the next visual, she would try to remove the acetate from the overhead projector by grabbing at the screen. The screen of course carried only a projected image of her transparency. Even funnier, is that she did this four times in a row.

If you are using an overhead, don't use the reveal method, using a sheet of paper to cover up certain bullet points that have not yet been discussed. The reason is that the audience will ponder, "Hey, I wonder what's under that sheet of paper?" rather than focus on your important message.

You won't need to cover anything up if you use the Absorb, Align, and Address method.

On the other hand, the reveal method is not necessary for today's high-tech presentations delivered from laptop computers, because the various bullet points can appear one row at a time.

A sheet of paper isn't needed and no one will wonder about what's hidden in the hard drive of a computer, because the next bullet point is not physically under any cover. The audience will know that it's coming up and they'll wait for it to pop into view.

Part Five

Odds and Ends

Hi-Tech Presentations

Today, with the availability of marvelous software and graphics packages, portable computers, and powerful projectors the possibilities for us as presenters are endless.

We are able to create incredible slides within seconds and able to do numerous things like import pictures, change backgrounds, use an array of sounds, incorporate animation, and pretty much produce anything that our minds want to create.

But with this incredible innovation come some challenges.

For one, I've been to so many presentations over the last few years where the people in the audience are more interested in getting their computer and software programs to perform the same functions as the speaker, than actually listening to what the speaker has to say.

After the presentation, the questions and comments don't revolve around, "How will we accomplish this together?" or "What an informative presentation!" but rather, "How did you get that bullet point to fly in there like that?" and "Which version of this do you need to create that?"

Suddenly, your electronic extravaganza has overshadowed your message, and you've become less interesting than your graphics.

Make sure that your hi-tech presentation assists you in making your point, but you don't want it to take away from you and your message.

Too many sounds, too much movement, and too many fancy tricks will only serve to distract. Remember to Keep It Super Simple, even when it comes to computer designed graphics; the same principles still apply.

A cordless mouse just like a cordless slide changer will make it easier for you to present. With these devices you are not confined to staying close to the computer or projector.

Don't be tempted to play with your remote mouse or slide changer though. These items can trigger the "magnet" problems we discussed earlier. Keep this device on a table or taped to the bottom scroll of the screen.

If you must hold this device, do so in one hand only. Avoid playing "hot potato" or becoming fidgety.

Finally, the more gadgets you use, the more susceptible you become to goof-ups. Have a back up plan ready. We don't want to see you spending the first 10 minutes of your presentation trying to reopen a file or reboot your computer.

I always carry hard copies (transparencies) of all my computer-generated visuals with me and I always have a flip chart in the room with markers, if all else fails.

This new technology is absolutely wonderful, but it is not more important than you, what you have to say, or your audience. If you can't make a presentation without your laptop or software package, what message are you giving the audience?

Pointers Of Any Kind Aren't Necessary

After discussing visuals I often get questions about using pointers.

In a nutshell, if you manage your visuals correctly and if you incorporate the Absorb, Align, and Address method, you don't need any type of pointer or laser pointer.

The only time that I have ever encouraged someone to use a pointer, was when I worked with an oil company in Bakersfield, California. Because they used oversized three-dimensional relief maps to explain things to other petroleum engineers and geographers, it was the exception.

Pointers are curious and they present many problems.

I've seen people test the wooden ones for tension and actually break them in half during a presentation.

Some people put their pointer behind the back like Jimi Hendrix did with his guitar at Woodstock, to test for even more resistance. The classroom is not a time for stress tests.

Still others end up waving the pointer, and the folks watching can't decide whether it's their old school principal or Lawrence Welk. You're not a conductor. You are a presenter.

The collapsible pointers are even more laughable because the presenter starts playing the pointer like an accordion, driving the audience crazy.

It is not advisable to put pens in the light of the overhead projection unit itself to point at a particular item. Often times the pen or pencil will roll off of the overhead or cover up words. I've also seen presenters poke or tattoo themselves with these writing utensils

Laser pointers are very popular these days, but the most interesting thing about them is that virtually no one in the audience likes them. The constant movement of light created by the laser pointer is frustrating for many and causes headaches for others.

If the visual is designed correctly, you won't need a laser pointer. If you must use one, use it judiciously and then either put it away in your shirt pocket or set it down somewhere because invariably you'll start playing with it if it stays in your hand.

The other problem with laser pointers is that even the steadiest of hands can't hold that thing still. Therefore even the slightest movement will indicate to the audience that you are nervous. It's a light show projecting exactly the wrong message.

If you absolutely insist on using a laser pointer, you may steady it somewhat by using both hands to hold it.

Podiums

Most people love the podium because they can hide behind it. Not only that, but they grab onto it and that podium is like 12,000 volts. Once someone grabs onto it, he or she just can't let it go.

Right away gestures are virtually eliminated and certainly any "aquatic" gestures (below the belt line) can't be seen because the podium hides them. Especially from behind the podium, your gestures must be enormous to get noticed.

Don't lean against the podium. Keep a nice balanced stance and move back from it.

By stepping back, the likelihood to lean and grab on to the podium will be greatly reduced and you will begin to look more comfortable.

Here is one idea that will set you apart from all other podium speakers!

If you're forced to speak from behind a podium, somewhere during the middle of your presentation or when you're about to elaborate on a point, walk away from the podium and stand before the audience. When you're finished making your point, come back to the podium. This will arouse your audience, as they will not be expecting this.

Think of one more time to walk away from the podium.

If you do this once towards the beginning and once towards the end of a twenty minute presentation, it can be a very effective way to liven up the room. Try it some time!

Microphones

At a presentation, which I attended in La Jolla, California, a speaker decided to call a break and go to the restroom. His cordless lavaliere microphone was still "live", the audiovisual person had left the ballroom, and the speaker was off to the restroom.

Most of the people who remained in the room heard the speaker make several off color candid comments and then listened as he did his business in the bathroom.

He returned to the room, receiving a standing ovation. When he realized what had happened, he almost fainted.

If you're speaking to 20 people or less, you generally don't need a microphone if you are able to project at the level 7-8 that you have been encouraged to do.

For larger audiences, cordless lavaliere microphones work the best, because a chord does not bind you and you don't have to hold it. This frees up both hands for gesturing. Just remember though, you may still be wearing it and it may still be on when you take a break.

Some microphones come attached to a podium. In this case, make sure the microphone is adjusted to where your chin is so that people can still see your face.

If you're planning on walking away from the podium, make sure that you have a cordless clip-on microphone, otherwise you'll have the wire yank you right back to where you started.

A freestanding mike looks like you're working a comedy club, but fortunately you don't have to hold it, again freeing up both hands for gesturing.

The carry-around, cordless mikes, which I think Phil Donahue popularized years ago, are nice, if you want to be mobile and walk around. There's truly no need for that, however, unless you're doing a pilot for a new talk show. Having to hold the mike with one hand creates all kinds of problems with fiddling, shaking, and one sided, gesturing.

No matter which microphone you use, don't forget to maintain your voice inflection. When most presenters see a microphone they automatically lower their volume. That's O.K., but unfortunately voice inflection and passion is lost in the process.

Yes, you can lower your voice somewhat, but don't lose the peaks and valleys, and the texture in your voice. Maintain the inflection in your voice and make sure that we stay awake.

Physical Skills in Different and Smaller Settings

What about utilizing physical skills and Absorb, Align, and Address in different or smaller settings?

Whether sitting down at a conference table or just one-on-one, the basic skills that you've read about so far apply just the same. But they have to be adapted to the various environments.

Eye contact is always a good thing regardless of how many people are listening to you.

A balanced stance means feet firmly on the ground. Remember not to cross one leg over the other. If you want to cross your legs, do so at the ankles. We don't want to distract from our message.

Gestures will be the same only smaller in size. If you talk about a big opportunity and you're sitting across the table from someone and you stretch both of your arms out as far as you can like an airplane, that may be too much and you may scare your listener into thinking that you need decaf. Just scale your gestures back.

On the other hand, I once heard a man present to a group and talk about his company being global. He was in front of a large group and he used a gesture to describe this. It was as if he was holding a tennis ball with both hands.

The lesson here: adjust the size of the gestures to the size of the audience. His gesture emphasizing the word global, might have been appropriate for a smaller group, but not for the several hundred listening.

Your vocal volume may drop to a 4 or 5 (roughly half of what it should ideally be in front of a large group), but don't make the common mistake of losing the passion/excitement/voice inflection just because the volume comes down.

The principles of Absorb, Align, and Address work in essentially the same way, even in smaller settings when using handouts. Your handout essentially becomes your visual and is placed on your left when you're sitting across the table from someone.

You still should manage your visuals and control the flow of information just as before when visuals are up on a screen.

Handouts and Props

It's O.K. to use props or handouts, but it's typically something you'll want to save until the end of your presentation because whatever object you hand out arouses curiosity in the audience and therefore becomes a distraction.

If you give somebody something to look at that they haven't seen before, you have effectively erased yourself from the room. But there's hope.

I highly recommend that you distribute handouts after your presentation is over. If people have something in their hands or on their desk they will look at it and then flip to the last page hoping that you'll get to where they are as soon as possible.

Since people read and peruse a document much faster than you can talk about it, not saving a handout until the very end guarantees that you will be out of synch with your audience. They are looking at one thing, and you are talking about another. You are essentially on two different pages.

If for whatever reason you must go through a handout before the end of your talk, guide your audience through it in a firm but friendly manner. Use people's names (if possible), refer to specific page numbers, and identify graphs and bold-faced passages, so your audience can follow you.

Something like, "There's a lot to cover here so please follow along with me if you would. Kevin; see there on page 3…Now if you'll look at the bottom of page 5 Lori, you'll see the graph and that blue line going up…The top of page 8 Ed, clearly outlines our objectives in bold faced print…

If you've elected to do it this way, you'll want to have a copy of the handout in your hands, while walking your listeners through it. By having an exact copy of what the audience has, you will make it easier to direct and control their attention.

Make sure your copy of the handout is clearly marked for you to follow, with paperclips sticky-pad sheets, whatever. You may write in transition statements on your copy, but know exactly where you are going and where you are going to take us. Have it clearly mapped out ahead of time.

Failure to do so or not understanding the flow of your own materials can become extremely embarrassing and you'll lose your audience and your believability. If you can't understand the flow of your materials, how can anyone else?

Handling props effectively requires the same logical skills with some added suggestions.

If you were to unveil a new product for example you might talk about it first, show pictures of its development, and talk about marketing and demographics. Then you might say something like, "Are you ready to see the_____?" Then you unveil it and everybody looks at it.

That's how they do it at car shows all of the time when new models are introduced to dealers, salespeople, and ultimately the general public. Talk about it first, give us some background, generate excitement; and then show us!

Overheads and Projectors

No matter what type of equipment you choose to use, make sure that it is in working order ahead of time, and make certain that the cables are all taped down so that you don't trip and fall.

Resist the temptation of leaning on the equipment or holding on to it during your presentation.

When using an overhead you can typically leave the visual on the projector once you've "removed the curiosity". Some people like to cover the visual back up by using a "flipper" which covers the light projection mechanism. An alternative would be to simply cover the visual or glass plate with a piece of cardboard.

If your presentation isn't that long anyway and you've got just a handful of slides, you might as well leave the light exposed and projecting on the screen. There is need to worry about being a light monitor and fumbling around to turn the switch on and off. Besides, turning the projector on and off will only serve to distract and it will burn out your bulb.

Some people like to leave notes near the overhead or on the overhead projector stand or table. Keep in mind that you have visuals to guide you through your presentation. You really don't need notes.

Having notes there in front of you will tempt you to look down and not at the audience. The audience will soon discover that you're reading not presenting and bad habits will start undermining your presentation.

Occasionally I'll get someone in one of my classes who insists on having his security blanket (notes) in front of him. I will ask him just for the heck of it to try his presentation without the notes, and offer him an extra practice session if he would, in fact, like to try again.

Invariably, it works out fine without the notes. But if you insist on having them, just make sure that you don't speak to them. That's the pitfall.

Flip Charts

Because of today's laptops and because of so many wonderful graphics programs that are available, flip charts are dying in popularity, however they can be useful when conducting workshops and as a back up system when all else fails. Like a flashlight or a flare, it's always good to have one around just in case.

If it's a straight presentation, you really don't need a flip chart. Most other visual delivery mechanisms (slide projectors, laptop projectors, and overhead projectors) simply work better and display your visuals more effectively.

But if you're trying to come up with ideas together as a group, and if you're asking the audience a lot of questions, flip charts work well.

If you need a "parking lot" page to list questions that can't be addressed during the session, but need to be documented, flip charts are effective also.

Flip charts work great in smaller groups if you're trying to explain a process, but there is really no use for flip charts in groups of 50 or more because not everyone will be able to see the writing on the pages.

When using flipcharts use thick pads. I typically leave at least one blank page in between each usable page to reduce the chance of marker ink bleeding through.

As with designing visuals, keep it super simple, be colorful, and write out the information big enough so that everyone can see.

Make sure that your flip chart is compatible with the number of pegs on the flip chart stand or that the clamp will hold your chart. Take masking tape along (always a good idea anyhow) just in case.

Many flip chart stands don't have a solid backing to write on since they are simply easels.

The main problem is that these types of easels are flimsy and don't provide a stable enough backing for you to write on.

Stand to the left side of the chart as the audience sees you and don't talk to the chart while writing. Stop, pause, and look at the audience to speak, but turn to the flip chart in silence to write. Since you're not writing a novel, this shouldn't be a problem.

Keep each page covered until you discuss it, and feel free to use your left hand to guide us through the flipchart visual using those same principals of Align, Absorb, and Address. It's always a great way to manage a visual, no matter what it is.

Bring and use different colored markers. Keep in mind that just plain old black markers are boring, and that red markers make us feel like school children that are about to get their papers corrected.

Mix it up a little with purples, greens, oranges, and blues. Typically pink and yellow are more difficult for the audience to see.

There are two methods by which you can make yourself aware of what's coming up on the next flip chart page.

Using the first method you simply bend the pages of the bottom left corner to offset the page, which is coming next. In pencil you may write on the corner, and those essentially become notes or reminders.

Others take sticky-pad sheets and stick them on all flip chart pages that will be used and write their notes on the sheet facing outward towards them.

I prefer bending the bottom part of the page because it looks a little cleaner to me than having flags of sticky-pad sheets hanging from the flip chart.

Either systems works fine and it is all a matter of personal choice.

The other advantage with flip charts is that you can write notes in pencil anywhere on the paper, and it cannot be seen by anyone but you. So if you want to dazzle your audience by remembering lots of facts and figures that's one way to do it.

Of course, look at your listeners when you speak and avoid turning your back to the audience.

Reading A Script and Using Teleprompters

Years ago I worked with a politician who confessed to me that he had to read a 20 page script and for whatever reason his script had been erroneously printed out because page 13 appeared twice in a row while page 14 had been lost. So essentially because it was prepared at the last minute, this particular politician grabbed the script and began reading it eloquently word for word, page after page.

Half way through the second reading of page 13, he realized that he was reading the same page again. But not to worry, because out of the several hundred people present, no one even noticed.

What does that tell you? First, no one listened and second, no one cared because the speaker was obviously reading a script.

Reading a script word for word is one of the most boring things you can do to an audience. And there are really very few who do it well.

Everyone notices that you're reading, and it lacks the freshness and excitement of a more spontaneous address. However, certain forums may require you to use this format, so if you're not able to use visuals or notes, you need to be prepared for script reading and/or teleprompting skills.

A Presidential State of the Union address, company annual meetings, and many more traditional types of settings occasionally require the use of script reading.

Teleprompters are becoming more available than ever and that's certainly the preferred way to go because it makes the audience feel like you're looking at and talking to them, even though they probably know that you're reading. We'll discuss teleprompters a little later.

The problem with script reading is that everyone knows that you're reading it. Many people start to question if you even wrote the speech yourself. Then the next thought is, "If she's just reading the script, why should I even listen to this? I could just read it myself."

Additionally, most speeches that are written don't read like you would normally speak. This causes voice inflection to go down, eye contact to be virtually non-existent, and your audience to tune out. Most script reading speakers become flat and boring.

Remember, great news writers for TV anchormen write for listeners not readers. It's not the same style as writing for the newspaper when you're speaking in public or reading in public for that matter.

It's important not to write to impress by using big words and stilted rhetoric that you normally wouldn't use. Tell the truth and be straightforward, don't be verbose. Use the words that you would normally use when you make a presentation. People can tell if it is not really you.

If you let someone else write your speech be absolutely certain that your speechwriter understands your personality, your style, and what you want to say. They must know your true voice.

If they don't, I'd suggest working very closely with them and giving them your undivided input. If you don't feel comfortable with a script and it's something that you can't really put your heart into, the audience will feel it.

If you choose to read a script word for word, make sure that your script comes prepared in large bold-faced script, which is similar to what you see newscasters wade through after a telecast.

This large bold print should be in large type using upper and lower case as you normally would and requires that you double space between lines and triple-space between paragraphs, but only use the top two-thirds of the page. This will keep you from dropping your chin.

You should arrange one or two vertical columns on normal sized paper, and make sure that you place only 5 words or fewer per line. Two vertical columns on one page are even more desirable than one because you won't have to turn as many pages.

Script Reading:
Create Two Vertical Columns

With these vertical columns, your eyes will move up and down without jumping back and forth from left to right. It avoids the problems associated with a horizontal layout, which makes it harder for the reader to grip a group or bracket of words. If you have 10-15 words per line and 25-30 lines per page, it would be very easy to lose your place.

The page number should be on the top and bottom of each page, and each vertical column should end with a period. Your script should be marked with slash marks, brackets, or different colored highlighters indicating the number of lines that you think you can recall when looking down at the page for a moment.

So, in essence the speaker looks down at several lines in silence, and then delivers those words to an audience member verbatim. Then she looks back at the several lines that she thinks she can absorb in one glance, and continues on through the entire script.

As you get used to this method you may be able to remember whole clusters or groups of words, above and beyond what you are normally comfortable with.

It's wise to paperclip your speech and not staple it. Once done with the page you can simply set it aside on the podium. No need to turn it over or put it back under the original stack of papers. It causes too much fumbling around.

Avoid the pit falls of typical script reading which is to eliminate eye contact with the audience all together, and to drag everyone along in an endless monotone of stale, scripted, read words, while leaning against the podium.

When using this script reading technique, remember to lock in all of the podium platform skills that we've already discussed. Just to reiterate, Lock, Talk, and Pause, raise your volume and inflection levels, and gesture above the belt line. "Aquatic" gestures will sink you for sure in this scenario.

You can make notes to yourself on your script as to when you should gesture and what type of gesture to use for a specific word or passage in the text. I use this technique frequently with executives and it has proven to be very effective.

Teleprompting skills are very similar but you have an advantage because one glass plate (2 total) is placed on each side of you, and you look directly at the audience when you look at your script. This avoids the hassle of having to look down at your notes and worry about memorizing a group of words before looking back out at the audience.

The teleprompter is actually very easy to read and is similar to script reading in that you will be reading vertical columns, which in this case are projected simultaneously onto both glass plates.

There's no fumbling around with pages, however, and most all teleprompter operators will follow the speaker's natural rhythm and pace. Make sure and practice with your teleprompter operator, so you get the hang of it. Hey, if all those rock stars and celebrities can use a teleprompter during those award shows, you can do it too.

In either case (script reading or teleprompter reading), there is an incredible temptation for people to speed up their delivery. This stems, from the fact that adrenaline is rushing through the body and the excitement propels you to read faster since the words are right there in front of you. And most people would reason that the faster they read, the sooner they get to sit down or go home.

It is imperative that you slow down during any presentation, but especially when you're reading a script or reading the teleprompter because it allows you to pause and look at the script below, or transition to the plate on the other side.

The real key in reading the teleprompter is that you pause, and in silence look at the other glass plate. It's got to be smooth.

Real teleprompting pros lock in and focus on various members of the audience as they transition from plate to plate; and they take their time. They also make sure to spend an equal amount of time looking at both glass plates (essentially both sides of the room), so that no one feels neglected.

Alternatives to Visuals, Scripts, and Teleprompters

Visuals eliminate the need to read notes and effective script reading or using a teleprompter may help out in the same way. But what other alternatives do you really have? There are basically two. A rough outline (or key word script) and a memory map (or pictograph).

If you will be using an outline or a memory map, and you have no visuals, this is the one time that I would strongly urge you to use a podium. If you don't use a podium in these two instances, you will be clutching on to your notes or pages in the fig leaf position, and it will not look right to your audience.

Everyone has a different way of organizing outlines, so organize your notes/outline in a way that makes sense to you.

You know the content better than anybody and your key word script, outline, or notes will probably not need to be longer than one page, unless you're planning a really long presentation that would probably require visuals anyway.

Just as with script reading, you will be tempted to look down at the words and read to your notes. Don't. Pause, take in the written cues that you have created for yourself and then look at one pair of eyes in the audience and deliver your message.

If you lose your train of thought, no problem, simply look down at your notes, in silence; pause, slow down, and then reconnect with the audience when you're ready.

Although, we typically don't have as much time to practice as we would like for any type of presentation, this is one time when I would strongly recommend you make time to rehearse. Just the idea of talking without a word for word script or the help of visuals may feel awkward at first, and therefore may require some getting used to.

You'll find that using an outline, notes, or a key word script is really not that difficult. The few words or phrases that you've written down will undoubtedly trigger your memory and you'll have no trouble finding the words to say, once you get started.

With a memory map or pictograph you're basically creating a visual or road map for yourself. You may also use this system in conjunction with key words or outlines. That's up to you.

The memory map is a concept based on the principle, which has been discussed in various parts of this book, that we remember visual images better than words and sentences.

Just like having words to look at to jar your memory, the memory map simply uses pictures in place of words to help you remember the points of your presentation. Because "a picture is worth a thousand words" the theory is that a few sketches or some computer-generated graphics will help remind you of your story line or idea, and the means of expression you want to employ.

A memory map is a one-page visualization of a presentation to aid the presenter in remembering what to say. It also forces you to work on one single surface, whereby you can see an overview of your entire presentation, essentially the "big picture".

Since memory maps are sometimes difficult to explain in the classroom, I usually create one in my seminars on a giant flip chart by asking the class to collectively decide upon a topic we can all agree to talk about.

After we've decided on the topic, I start creating icons and pictures in a logical pattern (almost like a game board) that might represent a point of view.

Then we discuss the page and when everyone seems to feel comfortable with it, I ask my students to memorize the images on the flip chart in their minds.

After this, I cover the sheet of paper and ask several students to come up and discuss our topic.

Invariably it's not difficult for them to do; in fact it's quite easy. The students more or less discover together as a group that they probably don't even need a script or notes. If they jot down a few pictures, and visualize and memorize, they can probably speak off the top of their heads. That's the power of a memory map.

If you absolutely must have an outline, key word script, memory map, or pictograph, but don't have a podium, you can put a sheet on the edge of a desk or on the floor (if you're up on a platform).

Make sure that your words and images are big enough to see and that you don't get caught reading to your notes. Again, I would prefer you not do this, but I want to give you some alternatives.

A Word about Preparation

When I was on the high school varsity tennis team I observed some interesting things about preparation and practice.

All of us on the team practiced a lot. We had to because we were in an extremely competitive league in Southern California, where the tennis talent is endless. Nevertheless, our team ended up clinching our league title and my partner and I won The Orange League Doubles Championships.

I noticed that the top players on our team never practiced too much the day before a match. They were well prepared, but they wanted to be fresh.

On the other hand, the guys that stayed long after practice was over and then came out early for more on the day of our matches always seemed to "choke" during the actual match.

Maybe they were tired? Perhaps they didn't feel invigorated? Maybe they couldn't handle the pressure of the big match and their long and extended practice and drill sessions were simply a way of compensating for their lack of mettle?

In any case, it was uncanny how the extra hard workers on the team would invariably lose their matches.

I remember years ago how tennis great John McEnroe said that he used to play doubles just to stay in shape and practice. He happened to be a great doubles champion as well and certainly blessed with tremendous talent, but when it came to match time he was "all business" and rose to the occasion, and usually won.

Perhaps he knew himself well enough to stay fresh for his matches.

So many training/presentations skills companies harp on how important preparation and practice are. I agree.

One company goes as far as even suggesting that you prepare a minimum of 30 hours before you give a 30-minute presentation. Let's consider this.

In a perfect world, that's not a problem. But what happens if your boss tells you that you have to give a speech before the end of the day, and it's now 11 AM and you still have a lot to do.

In this fast-paced world of global economy and e-business, who's got 30 hours to prepare for a presentation? No one! That's why long preparation is wishful thinking.

In addition, if you've had the luxury of long hours of preparation in the past, you will now panic if you suddenly don't have ample time to prepare.

Realistically, no matter how much time you've spent rehearsing, once you've been called to the stage, you'll start getting nervous and your knees will start shaking. All of those same fears will set in, whether you've rehearsed 3 hours or 300 hours. It won't make a difference.

Ultimately, you need to get a hold of yourself and apply your acquired skills to be a successful presenter. Trust in yourself and in your presentation skills techniques and the rest will fall into place.

Have the confidence to know that one more hour of preparation won't make a difference at this point because you've already put in the time. The curtain has been raised, you are as good or better than any other presenter out there, and it is now show time. Go for it!

Speaking On the Spot

What if you're asked to speak on the spot? Will you tell your boss, or your client, that you need thirty hours to prepare? You've just been called up to the podium, and here's a chance for you to really shine. What now?

I say, seize the opportunity!

This all reminds me so much of broken plays in football. The teams prepare for a certain play, but the play gets busted up during the actual game and it doesn't go as planned.

So, what do you do when you have the perfect game plan, but things don't go as planned? You improvise and make the best of it.

Former quarterback John Elway of the Denver Broncos made a career out of turning broken plays into touchdowns. He used his skill of evading tacklers to turn lemons into lemonade game after game. That's what the great ones do. They rise to the occasion.

Conversely, an interesting thing happened when Al Pacino won The Academy Award for Best Actor with his role in "Scent of a Woman."

During his acceptance speech, Mr. Pacino, who is obviously a first-rate actor, seemed incredibly nervous and uneasy as he worked his way through his fragmented speech.

This is a perfect example for me to share with you, because here's one of the world's best actors winning an award for best actor, but at this occasion he doesn't have a script.

Although genuine in his emotions, he seemed to be completely caught off guard by the award.

Sometimes we get thrown into that type of situation, and having the basic skills down will help you look credible under any circumstances, whether you've rehearsed (I would prefer that you do) or not.

Years ago, I was working for a major automotive manufacturer and was hired to take part in what is know as a Ride & Drive.

This is a traveling road show, designed to give sales people and managers a chance to drive, learn, and acquaint themselves with a new model which they will shortly be receiving in their showrooms to sell.

I've done a lot of consulting in the automobile industry because of my experience working in sales training and with dealerships. I was asked to do this Ride & Drive at the eleventh hour as the company facilitating the event was short-handed and their client had seen a video tape of me running a sales workshop.

I was assigned to do a "walk-around" presentation of the new vehicle that we were introducing, which means that I had to highlight and explain about 25 new features and engineering improvements.

With almost no time for rehearsal, the company asked us to do a dry run for the executives of the automotive company including the instructional designers who had developed and designed this particular Ride & Drive.

Naturally, I felt a tremendous amount of pressure because I had come in highly recommended, at the last minute, and had been assigned to do the most technical portion of the presentation, something I honestly did not feel completely comfortable with.

The plan was to hook me up with a cordless lavaliere mike, so I could highlight the different features of this new vehicle and elaborate on them as I walked around the car.

To make matters worse, a cameraman was to follow me with a digital camera so that my image would be projected on the giant screen behind me. I hadn't felt that much excitement since my Crazy Horse debut in May of '94.

I had literally a few hours to prepare. 30 hours were simply not available, but the company that had hired me along with the course designers and executives, naturally expected perfection.

Although I know a lot about cars, I am certainly not an engineer or technical expert, but I do understand presentation skills. Fortunately, I had a facilitator guide and was able to memorize a few key points and leave index cards hidden behind tires, the engine compartment, etc. to get me through the rest.

Well, my walk-around presentation was a big hit and led to many more automotive Ride & Drive assignments. Was it because I was knowledgeable about cars? Perhaps to some degree, but the fact that I had mastered the physical skills of presenting allowed me to succeed.

Obviously I spent every moment that I had prior to the "dry run" studying and preparing. The point is though, I knew the material, but I also looked good presenting it. That was an effective combination.

When I was still relatively new to training, I was sent to Phoenix, Arizona to do a one-hour workshop for an investment company at The Biltmore Hotel. Everything had gone wrong for me with this particular session.

My class materials had not arrived, the time of my session had been moved up, and my flight was late. As I arrived at the venue, I found out that I was not only going to be presenting earlier than expected, but that the person ahead of me was cutting into half of my time.

So, I only had a half an hour to present, although I had been scheduled for one. Of course the people at the event were expecting a lot from a presentations skills expert and the company that had sent me out on this assignment was still evaluating my progress, as it was still my trial period.

A few minutes after arriving at the main ballroom of The Biltmore and without warning, I was introduced to approximately 1,000 people. I designed my speech in my head as I walked to the front of the room.

I knew the subject matter, so I simply decided to talk about everything relative to presentation skills. I locked in my presentation skills techniques and took command of the room.

I was scared to death, but no one knew and no one could tell. My presentation went over so well that I was asked to do several more for this company.

The company that had set up the meeting was delighted and asked me to do many more engagements for them thereafter.

Now, these are not "Gee, isn't Till Kahrs wonderful stories".

The point is that here are two examples of me being thrown, completely unprepared into chaotic circumstances, but I managed to succeed and surpass audience expectations.

No it's not that I'm brilliant, because I'm not, but it's because I had a command of some basic physical skills. That's all. If I can succeed in these environments, so can you.

Would you panic if you had lunch with a friend and they asked you to brief them or give them an update on something? No! You know the subject matter and "off the cuff", you could deliver that information without a hitch. Why? Because you're not afraid and you do know the information.

In the same way, it's no different in front of a large room. The only difference is that there are more people, so you Lock, Talk, and Pause just like you've already learned to do.

How to Practice

Years ago, I saw legendary singer Percy Sledge at the annual Blues Festival in San Francisco. He of course is the singer who made the mega-hit "When a Man Loves a Woman" world-famous.

Somewhere during the middle of his set he remarked, "My Moma' once told me 'You gotta' know your thang' before you do it.'" I couldn't have said it better.

Should you practice and is practice a good thing? Obviously, yes you should practice, but how?

Best thing to do is stand in your room, office, hotel and look at different objects in the room, pretending that these various objects are people and pairs of eyes.

Start practicing and get into that rhythm of moving from person to person, with the flowerpot, the remote, the paperweight, whatever object happens to be available.

Also use a mirror to practice Absorb, Align, and Address, and only speak when you look yourself in the eye.

Rehearse your presentation as often as possible, but more importantly have the skill set locked in that will help you deliver the message. Going back to the football analogy. What's the point of having a game plan or strategy to beat the other team, if your players don't know how to block and tackle?

If you know how to block and tackle then at least you have a chance to execute your game plan, no matter what unexpected things might happen. You must have ownership of the basic physical skills and if you do, you'll be able to succeed and survive under pressure.

Dress

Early in my training career, I was addressing a group of employees at a credit card company in San Diego, California.

Right before the last student had arrived and the class was about to begin, I bent over to pick up a misplaced workbook, and that was it…my pants split from seam to seam, front to back.

It was too late to do anything about it, my timing was terrible, but the show had to go on.

So I buttoned my suit jacket, lengthened my tie slightly, and promised myself not to turn my back to the audience while wearing my jacket extra low in back.

It worked and I got through the day without a problem. Fortunately, I was not exposed.

Ironically, at the end of the day my class was filling out comment cards, when all of a sudden someone said, "You know Till, you look pretty comfortable up there, tell us about the most embarrassing thing that's ever happened to you."

I thought about it for a moment. This had been a very young, fun, and lively bunch so I told them, "Well, you wouldn't believe what happened to me today."

As I slowly lifted up my jacket to expose my blunder, I began doing a model runway turn and continued, "I bent over to pick up a work book and I split my pants from seam to seam, just this morning."

The group roared!

Sometimes people wear old clothes or new clothes that either represent better days gone by or wishful thinking. The problem is that everyone can see the clothes don't fit. So wear comfortable clothes that fit.

Some general rules about style. When in doubt, be on the conservative side, and here's why.

It's easier for me to role up my sleeves and take my tie and jacket off, if I appear too formal at a presentation. But, if I'm wearing shorts and a golf shirt and everyone is wearing a suit and tie, what am I going to do? Going from conservative to casual is easier to do than the other way around.

Other guidelines suggest that you always dress a notch up from your audience. This shows your professionalism and it's a good basic rule.

How often has someone said, "That presenter simply looked too well-manicured and too well put together." On the other hand, you don't want to overdo things and appear slick. Safest is to match the style of your audience.

For the guys, if it's a suit and tie crowd and you're giving a presentation of an hour or less, then I would leave your jacket on. I suggest that you leave your jacket buttoned during the first minute or so. You can always loosen up the jacket later.

If I'm doing a full day session wearing a suit and tie, the jacket's usually off by the afternoon. Start formal, then loosen up a bit if that feels right.

Since I've been teaching training seminars around the beginning of 1990, the dress code for business has changed dramatically. It is the rare occasion now that I wear a suit.

It seems that business casual is here to stay. And my clients request it time and time again for either keynote speeches or full length training sessions.

There are also regional differences. Generally speaking, people and companies are more conservative the further east you travel. But the rule here about dress is that there are no rules or constants.

As part of your audience analysis, make sure you know what the audience will be wearing. Always ask the client or person setting up the meeting about their recommendations for dress.

I typically say something like this to the individual or individuals hiring me, "…and on the subject of dress, I've got everything in my closet from suits and tuxedos, to khaki pants and golf shirts. Do you have a preference or recommendation? What ever works best for you is great with me. You know this group better than anyone."

They appreciate you asking, it shows that you're a pro, and in this way you'll know the drill ahead of time.

The reason I say that there are no rules anymore relative to dress is because with some high-tech companies the formal more conservative approach may not be fashionable.

Conforming to traditional ways may be a mistake in these circles. It all depends on the corporate culture, the audience, and your good judgment. So, when in Rome…

For the ladies, I would recommend not wearing too much jewelry. The jewelry can become a distraction for you and the audience, especially if you're gesturing or using the principles described in Absorb, Align, and Address.

And if etiquette falls under the subject of dress, obviously chewing gum or eating food while speaking is a definite no-no. But a sip from a beverage if your speech is over 20 minutes long, is certainly more than acceptable.

Just remember to slow down, take a deep breath, and comfortably enjoy your beverage. I've seen far too many drinks knocked over or spilled, by speakers who were just starting to loosen-up.

What's The Best Time of Day to Present?

Mid-morning, about 10AM is the most ideal time of day to make a presentation. Since it's not too early, people have now woken up and you have their attention.

The worst time is right after lunch, during a meal, or during cocktail hour because you're competing with naptime, food, or drinks.

Obviously, being the last speaker to go on after a full day of speeches can be troubling, but please don't say, "I know you're probably not listening anyway at this point." Take the opportunity to wake everybody up, so they are glad to have stayed until the very end.

Regardless of the time slot you draw, you should always seize the moment and shake up your audience. They won't expect to be awoken from an afternoon nap, the complete sedation by the last speaker, or the wear and tear of an all-day event.

If you are a dynamic speaker, it doesn't really matter what time of day you present. And if you draw the 10AM slot, you're a double winner

The Day of the Event

Several years ago in Philadelphia I had an engagement with an electronics manufacturer. I had showed up early, everything had checked out O.K., and I started my presentation.

I was using slides and I was using a cordless slide changer. Unfortunately, it seemed as though I had no control over the slide projector and my slides would randomly move forward and back without me pressing one button.

I was truly perplexed and just assumed there was a ghost in the machine.

I was just about ready to turn off my uncontrollable slide projector, when in walked a presenter from the room next store and asked, "Are you having trouble with your slide projector also?"

After a few minutes of discussion, we determined that both of us were on the same frequency with our cordless remotes, therefore we were advancing each other's slides, without even knowing it.

The frequencies were changed and we went on with our respective classes.

Anything can happen out there, yet there's never a reason to panic.

Always show up at least one hour before the event starts, two hours to be extra sure.

Invariably things will go wrong for you when you are presenting, especially if it's not your own backyard or office. There's always something to fix or straighten out. I can tell you this from personal experience.

By showing up early you get comfortable with the room, and hopefully you'll have enough time to handle any problems. Always check out and try all of the audiovisual equipment. It doesn't matter who said that it's working until you see it with your own eyes.

Once the class starts and something doesn't work, the participants won't care that the banquet manager told you an hour ago that the equipment was in fact working. It's your responsibility to check out every detail and every last piece of machinery.

When dealing with banquet managers and/or support staff, be pleasantly persistent if you have a problem. You want to let everyone know that your presentation has top priority and that if there is something wrong, it needs to get fixed immediately. You don't, however, want to become obnoxious. There's a way to be firm, without going over the line.

Remember that the people in charge of your room are making your lunch too and that you may need their help later. They also may work for your client or contact and report your unacceptable behavior. Be professional, persistent, but be pleasant.

If you're having problems getting something done, go up the chain of command, so that everyone knows you mean business. After your event is over, thank everyone for his or her help and leave a good impression. You may see them again before too long.

When at a hotel or office always get the name and extension of the individual in charge of the operation and the name and extension of the audiovisual department. This can be a lifesaver if something goes wrong, and always ask for or carry a spare bulb for a slide or overhead projector.

When something goes wrong during your presentation and it will, call a short break and handle the situation. Don't panic about anything! As long as you're alive and the office or hotel you're in is not burning-it'll pass and you'll get by. Believe me, I've seen just about everything including rats in the back of the room.

Make sure that the lights aren't turned down too low. Yes, your audience needs to see the slide on the screen, but they also need to see you.

To that end make sure that hanging-lights or chandeliers don't get in the way of your screen. Also, check to see if the chairs right in front of your projector won't project images of people's heads. You may need to raise the projector or move the chairs.

If you use a podium, make sure that the podium has a light. If it doesn't make sure it's well lit so you can view the notes or pictures that you place down.

Find out who'll be presenting in the room next to you. It's tough to compete with the local beauty pageant or a wrestling competition. Move your venue if you need to (another reason to show up early).

Have only a few, with heavy emphasis on few, extra chairs if you know exactly how many people are coming to your event. Too many empty chairs make you look bad and chairs can be very easily removed before anyone even shows up.

Standing room only makes you look good.

Keep in mind also that people never sit in the front rows first (it's never happened to me in over ten years). So if you have extra rows of chairs in the front and many people don't show up, the first few rows will be completely empty.

It's awkward speaking to a group when the first two rows are not filled. It's even more difficult to ask people to move up a few rows once they've sat down. Break down "the wall of chairs" between you and the audience.

Classroom style seating is generally the way to go, especially if you're presenting to large groups of people.

In a smaller group, a U shaped seating arrangement or conference table is fine, but it's easier to feel 'closer' to everyone, in a classroom style environment with an aisle down the center of the room. If you have the option, and you usually do, use a classroom style seating arrangement.

Make sure that any chords are taped down with duct tape or electrical tape. I've seen many a presenter (me included) or participant trip over wires, knock down equipment, and fall flat on their face. It's embarrassing for everyone.

Are their ventilation problems in your room?

See what you can do to open some windows or turn on the air conditioning unit. It's difficult to find a temperature level that suits everybody, but generally speaking cold is better than hot.

You don't want a meat locker, but a cooler temperature will keep your audience awake. No one goes on vacation to a tropical island to work. As much as I like drinks with umbrellas, it's not for my classes.

When speaking in a hotel or convention center, always check to see that your event is posted at the entrance of your venue. Will people know where to go?

I can't tell you how many times I've checked the marquis or the signage, only to find my name is misspelled, the name of the seminar or company is wrong, or no one has listed the room or floor number.

If it's a big place you may even have to post your own signs and tape them to the wall, marking safe passage to your event.

For presentation purposes, many hotels will assemble a platform for you to stand on. Test the ramp or steps that lead you to the platform. Often times these devices are wobbly and unsteady. Walk around on the platform a few times to determine if it squeaks and make sure it is stable.

I had one platform collapse on me while I was walking on stage. Make certain that you're on sure footing, literally.

In today's advanced age of telecommunications, almost everyone has a cell phone and/or pager. Please indicate to all participants that these devices should be placed on vibrate or pulsate mode only.

If you do not make this announcement at the very beginning of your engagement, guaranteed interruptions and distractions will occur. Most audience members will also consider cell phone and pager noise to be rude and annoying.

Obviously, I've had the opportunity to make many presentations. Please learn from my mistakes and the experience of others.

Beforehand and Loosening-Up

Public speaking is performance art and you need to warm up before the show.

One of the best things you can do to loosen-up is greeting people when they come in to see you. This is something that I've practiced over and over again. It has consistently worked wonders for me and I highly recommend it to you.

I always extend a hand, smile, make direct eye contact and welcome my guests. I let them know where the restrooms are, we chit chat a little, and I try to find out about them. This helps me get my motor started and they get to know me.

By the time my class starts my voice is warm, they feel more comfortable about me, and I'm ready to roll.

Obviously, I understand that you can't always meet and greet your guests before a speech. Sometimes you'll be on a panel or sitting at a table. Other times you'll be pacing around backstage waiting to get on.

Wherever you are and whatever situation you are in, I do recommend that you talk to whoever is around you. It will help you relax and feel more comfortable, even if it's the soundman backstage or someone's family member sitting next to you.

Because you'll be nervous before any performance, let some of that steam out of your pot before you start your presentation by stretching, rolling your shoulders, walking around, taking deep breaths, whatever it takes to start the flow of that nervous energy outward.

Start your engine and press on the gas a little before you come barreling down the straightaway.

Introductions

I recently attended a pharmaceutical conference in Palm Springs, California. An elderly physician who was moderating gave me a glowing introduction. Everybody clapped, I was grateful for the kind words, and I walked up to the platform to speak.

The moderator went straight from the platform to his seat and put his head down before I even uttered my first word. I raised my volume, used gestures, and was really "on" that day, but the moderator never looked up once and went off to sleep.

As soon as I finished my presentation, he enthusiastically jumped out of his chair and shook my hand indicating, "Great job! Well done, Till."

This had to be one of the weirdest things that I've ever seen.

I've heard some undesirable introductions in my life, but two stand out.

In the mid-eighties, when I was still in the beverage industry, I attended a cocktail reception in New York City. A lobbyist representing our company introduced a senator stating, "This is my dear long time friend who I know so well…" and then he paused for what seemed like a half a minute to pull an index card out of his pants and introduced the senator by name.

Some of us had already had a few drinks because the senator had arrived late, and we couldn't contain our laughter.

On another occasion someone introduced a keynote speaker by saying, "This man needs no introduction..." (which is an overused phrase) and then proceeded to give the longest introduction that anyone had ever heard.

When the speaker finally arrived on the platform, people cheered wildly, not for the speaker, but because they were so relieved that the boring, long-winded introduction had finally ended.

So, what is a good introduction? Simply put, short and sweet and building the speakers' credibility with the audience. You don't want to steal the presenters' thunder, but you do want to whet the audience's appetite.

Something like, "Our next speaker is a decorated war veteran who saw active combat on many occasions and who is now able to share with you today what he has learned from his experiences. Please welcome Bob Johnson."

If you know that you will be introduced, make it easy for your emcee or moderator and write out a brief introduction or give them your abbreviated BIO. Up to 1 minute is fine, but a ten-minute introduction is too long, and the audience will have fallen asleep before the featured speaker even starts.

Whenever I give an intro or BIO to someone they're extremely grateful. It makes it easy on them and makes me look professional.

Once introduced, it's always nice to thank the person and/or audience for having you. I can't imagine why you wouldn't do it. It's never wrong to be polite.

Part Six

Questions and Answers

Why Is This So Tough?

What makes Q&A so unique and difficult is that you never know what questions to expect.

When you give a presentation, you are fully in command of your audience. You know the subject matter and you have the physical skills locked in; you have control. And in front of a room that's a nice place to be.

However, when you open yourself up for questions, everything changes because you don't know what your listeners will ask. Someone may be trying to make you look bad or make you appear defensive. All of a sudden the world can become a very lonely place.

Getting Off On the Right Foot

There are ways to streamline the entire Q&A process. This ultimately gives you more control, and presents you with some options.

When you start your presentation you can say, "I will be going through this presentation and I'd be happy to take your questions after my presentation is over." That way you kindly let your audience know that there will be a time for questions, but later.

This is typically the format for more formal style presentations where you have firm control.

On the other hand, you may want to encourage questions throughout your presentation, especially if you know it's friendly fire or you are in a classroom style environment.

Since I'm typically instructing, I will encourage questions throughout my two-day seminars. However, if it's a half hour keynote speech I will ask that the audience hold their questions until the break, or I may not even bring up the subject, since the format and my client simply won't allow for Q&A.

If someone inadvertently asks about Q&A, I'll address it then. Otherwise I won't even bring it up.

Some presentation skills coaches suggests that you always take questions right before you conclude your presentation so that the audience's questions have been answered and you end with your concluding remarks on an "emotional high note". Let's look at this logically.

You've got the audience in the palm of your hand, you're striding in full, and now you're going to stop dead in your tracks for questions where you have no control over what will be asked.

After you weather that storm, you start back up and conclude.

Sure it can work, if you're skilled and crafty at presenting, but may I strongly suggest that you finish your presentation first. Then take questions and using the powerful skill of rephrasing (which you will learn), end with yet another positive message, using the audiences' questions to tie back to your main point of view.

In this way you don't have to stop and start your engine. It's logical, it's clean, and it looks good!

Let's examine some of the possibilities that may occur if you stop for questions before your conclusion.

First, you may ask for questions and not get any, which may leave the impression that your speech was boring and non-inspiring (when in fact people are just afraid to ask).

Second you run the risk of getting a negative question, not knowing the answer, or having someone ask something that has nothing to do with where you want to go or how you want to conclude.

If you stop and ask for questions before you end your presentation, you're creating extra work for yourself that's simply not necessary.

Because we're out of control in the Q & A process, we have to find a way to structure the interaction so that you're back in control and so that you have the chance to manage the whole process. It's tough to do, but it can be done.

Before we discuss this method in detail always remember to never appear defensive or angry. We've all been tempted to lose our cool, but it's not worth it in the long run. Maintain your composure at all times, even when it's difficult.

This does not mean that you should be flippant or apathetic about a difficult situation, however, trust the techniques on the following pages to help guide you to safe passage.

It's also easy to forget all that we've learned about presentation skills when we get nailed with a tough question! We start scanning, fidgeting, and going back to our old crutches when we feel singled out and out of control.

We've learned about physical skills throughout this book and we need to continue to incorporate those lessons. But now we'll be focusing more on some verbal dexterity. It's difficult to use the two skill sets in tandem at first, but if you can master it, nothing looks better.

Let's examine a four-step method that will help you mange the Q & A process effectively, regardless of what type of group you are facing.

1) Raise Hand and Ask for Questions

Assuming you want to encourage questions, and again that's obviously dependent on the audience and what you're trying to accomplish, there are many ways to do so.

You can ask, "Are there any questions?" The problem here is that this is a closed-ended question and it's possible that someone says "no" or nothing at all.

More encouraging might be, "What questions do you have?" Even better, "At this point many people typically have questions. What questions do you have?" If that isn't inviting, I don't know what is.

To help you control the crowd you may want to raise your hand as you ask for questions because this encourages your audience to do the same. For larger crowd control purposes this is a very good idea because it's easier to pick from a bunch of raised hands than to have everyone clamoring for your attention.

This first step gives you control and sets up an order to the Q & A process that you will now be able to manage.

2) Select Someone and Listen

Next up you'll want to select someone by extending your arm with an open palm, and then; listen.

When choosing someone don't point at that individual. It just doesn't look right when you wag a finger. I'm amazed at how many people still point.

Should you use names? Well, the general rule is, unless you know everyone's name don't use names because you may show favoritism.

Of course, there are always exceptions. For example, your boss is in the room, or an important client just flew in from overseas to be at your presentation. Use good judgement, but it's easier to be consistent selecting with an open palm.

During Presidential press conferences favoritism is often times shown. The well known reporters will be allowed to sit in the front rows and are addressed by first name, but then the reporters trying to break into the elite group are simply asked, "Yes?"

That's Washington DC's political pecking order, but it doesn't apply to day in day out presentations for mainstream America.

Occasionally you'll hear a presenter say something like, "The young lady up front" or "The good looking guy in the back". That's dangerous for obvious reasons.

Now if everyone else you select isn't referred to as young or good looking what are the implications? That they're old and ugly?

Selecting someone with an open palm is a nice neutral way of choosing someone. It makes it easy on you and takes the pressure off. It's the safest easiest way to select and requires less thought. You need as few distractions as possible during the Q & A process.

After selecting someone, you must listen to the question. Most of us at this point are so eager to respond that we start tuning out the question and start formulating an answer.

Stop for a moment, make eye contact with the questioner, and listen to the question. Listen to the entire question. There'll be plenty of time to formulate an answer and respond, in spite of what you might think.

While listening, several unexpected things can happen that I'd like to address.

The questioner may start rambling on and on.

If this happens, give the questioner a fair chance. But if it runs too long kindly interrupt, raise your volume and say something like, "I can tell this question is important to you, can you give me the question as concisely as possible, that way I'll be able to take a few other questions. By the way, if you have any other questions after my presentation, please feel free to contact me."

In a nice way you're saying," I'm pleased about your excitement, but out of fairness to everyone else, shorten it up, but feel free to be in touch after all of this is over."

It's clean, diplomatic, and the audience typically will manage it from there, because they want a chance to ask questions too.

Sometimes someone will ask two questions at once.

You'll have the option here of answering only one question, answering both questions, putting the task on the speaker to remind you about the other question, or fusing the two questions together by effectively rephrasing.

More about rephrasing in just a moment.

If you don't understand the question put the onus on yourself. "I'm not sure I understand" or "Can you put that another way?" Never say, "Your question isn't clear" or "I can't understand that question".

It may be absolutely true that their question is unclear but put it on you. It looks better to everyone.

Sometimes, a questioner will make a statement and not even ask a question like "That idea just won't work!" Then you must retort back with, "I'm sorry, did you have a question?"

The other option is to rephrase this negative statement into a positive or neutral question like, "So why will this plan work and what will the benefits be to all of you?"

Often times I'll take control of the statement and rephrase at this point, especially if it's negative. If I give my questioner another chance to ask another question or make another statement, they may further try to berate me, so I usually go for the positive rephrase.

3) Rephrasing/Repeating (Optional)

Rephrasing or repeating is the next step in the Q & A process, but it's an optional step.

It's optional because the room may be small and it is not necessary to repeat every question. Keep in mind also that sometimes questioners are loud enough to where everyone does hear the question.

Repeating questions constantly can become monotonous to the audience. Any kind of repetitive behavior can get on your nerves just like using the same word over and over again.

However, rephrasing can save your life if you feel like you're in a shark tank and someone has just bitten one leg off and there's blood everywhere.

What if someone asks you, "Why does this cost so much?" or "Why did you fire all those employees?" Appropriate rephrases might be "What will the investment be?" and "Why did we restructure the company as we did?"

Q & A

• Rephrase (Optional)

- Helps Audience Hear Question
- Gives Speaker Time to Think
- Neutralizes Negative Question
  - For Example: "How much is this going to cost?"
  - Neutralized: "What will the investment be?"

The rephrasing step is like magic dust under those volatile conditions. Having the opportunity to neutralize any question or "diffuse the bomb", as I like to put it, gives you an incredible power and should arm you with extra confidence.

Sometimes my students will remark that rephrasing may appear slick or sneaky.

Here's the issue: If someone asks a biased question that's intended to injure my credibility in front of my peers, I want to be able to be in a position to respond effectively. And I tell my students, that you can always elect to repeat a negative question, if you'd like, but I'd like to have the option to rephrase, if I need to.

It's important to have this resource available, especially with a tough audience and/or a large crowd.

The other problem with repeating and not rephrasing a negative question is that it implies that it's true. For example if you repeat back, "So, why did we fire those people?" If that's what really happened and you want to take the moral high road, fine; but if it's not what happened it sure sounds to me like you fired some people.

Repeating or rephrasing has many great benefits!

It allows you extra time to think for a good answer and lets the audience hear what the question was. How many times have you been in a room and the presenter answers a question but no one knows what the questioner asked? It happens quite frequently.

One word of caution. When we get stung by a tough question, the tendency for us is to take a step back, look at the ceiling, or lower our heads. Our body language starts to show signs of uneasiness again. Since we've been put on the defensive, all of those negative bad habits start creeping back in and we go back to our old ways. Don't!

Slow down, lock in all of the physical skills we've learned up to this point, and step up your level of energy. End this Q & A session on a high note! Don't let a rough questions ruin it for you at this juncture. You've come too far to let your great impression slip away.

4) Answer and Tie Back

The final phase here in the Q&A process is to answer back to the questioner (always satisfy the original questioner first, out of courtesy) and then tie back your answer to your main idea if possible and put a positive spin on whatever it is you're trying to promote.

For example, someone asks you, "Why did you fire all of those people?" Your rephrase, "So why did we restructure the company? Well, in an effort to streamline our sales process and continue to be competitive we simply had no choice. During this process we've actually created more opportunities for growth in the company and as I mentioned during my presentation, sales have never been stronger and we have never been more profitable. That's why I know we did the right thing!"

Here, you've taken a negative question, neutralized it, and then answered in a positive way tying your answer pack to your original presentation. That's how a real pro does it.

If you elect to repeat or rephrase a question it's effective to look at someone other than the questioner. You will, however, want to give the beginning of the response back to the questioner before delivering the response to the whole room.

Keeping the rest of the audience involved with the Q & A process is critical to your success, and they'll help and support you in the process.

Finally, although many questions require longer answers, don't get in the habit of over-answering questions. Once you feel comfortable that you've answered the question, stop.

The excitement of a public forum may often times propel us to ramble and give longwinded answers. This can sometimes be interpreted as being defensive or pompous.

Should You?

Should you ever say "good question", after someone asks a question?

Generally speaking no, because if you say "good question" to one person, you'll have to say it to everyone. You should be consistent, otherwise you're indicating that one persons' question is good and someone else's isn't.

The exception of course is if you need to be politically smart. For example, if your boss or an important client asks a question, you might want to indicate that it's a good question, etc. On the other hand if our audience perceives you as "kissing up", you may lose trustworthiness. Use good judgement, as always.

When you do rephrase a question don't say, "He/She wants to know" or "The questions is…"The question is…. That gets old and it's repetitive.

Simply rephrase the questions with "why, how, are we, could we, did we, etc." Whatever they ask, just use a straight rephrase based on their question.

Don't defer the question to someone else unless you're absolutely sure that person is comfortable with answering that question and it's been discussed in advance. If that doesn't happen you can embarrass someone and make everyone look bad, especially yourself.

It's O.K. to defer occasionally, but if it's done too often in one session, people may start wondering, "Well what the heck is he up there for anyhow? Why doesn't he just let her answer the questions?" You may lose credibility.

As mentioned before, consider giving your initial response to the original questioner and then spread the rest of your answer randomly around the room. Audiences will love you for it if you include them and it helps you to avoid a confrontation with the one bad apple in the group.

For maximum control, never end your answer by looking at the original questioner because they'll hit you with a follow-up question. It's what I call the "Yea' but".

If you get a"yea' but" anyway when you end on someone else, I'll give the original questioner a second question or opportunity, but after that kindly remind him or her that others may have questions too.

The audience typically handles the rest. They also want to have the opportunity to ask questions and typically don't want one individual monopolizing the entire Q & A session.

If you're in a classroom environment you may actually want to end or give your entire answer to the questioner to make sure that they understood your answer. This may also be appropriate for the boss or an important client. You'll know when it's the right time.

Typically with a large crowd, new faces, and not much time to spare (a keynote, etc.), I end on someone other than the original questioner for maximum control.

When the president of the company who hired me for the engagement asks a question I may give him the entire answer. You obviously have some flexibility.

What Ifs

Sometimes your audiences will not be inspired to ask questions. What if you want the audience to ask questions and you ask for them in an open-ended way, and no one asks anything because of stage fright or lack of synergy?

I'll always have a few questions tucked away for an occasion like this and say something like, "You know the other day someone asked me…it was interesting because…" Then I'll try again to illicit questions. That'll do the trick 99% of the time.

If you try two or three times, volunteering your own questions and still no one is inspired to ask any questions, perhaps it's time to call it a day, head back to the hotel, order room service, and see what's on cable.

I've told my classes for years that if you don't know the answer to a question simply make eye contact, use gestures, raise your volume, use lots of voice inflection, and make up the answer. That gets about the biggest guaranteed laugh out of all the things I say, so I share it with you. Saying this with a straight face helps since it's obviously a joke.

Of course you should never make up an answer, or lie under any circumstances. If you don't know the answer to a question it's really important that you handle it correctly.

If you don't know an answer, don't get that panicked look on your face and start staring at the ceiling, while beads of sweat begin rolling down your face and say," Gee, I'm sorry I don't know".

Instead keep up your energy level and say something like, "I don't know the answer to that particular question, but if you'll check with me after this presentation, I'd be happy to get back to you on that".

Notice I say, "If you'll check with me". That puts the onus on the questioner to hunt me down because I may be pressed for time to make my connecting flight to the next seminar, but I need to give him a chance to find me.

I also suggest that, "I'd be happy to get back to you" which I will if he hunts me down, but I don't guarantee him an answer. I'll certainly try to find him an answer and I'm sure that I will, but I don't guarantee him anything that I can't deliver on. It's very critical that you don't over promise on something, especially in a public forum.

If you get two questions that are not answerable you may want to consider winding up your presentation and quit while you're ahead, unless the purpose of your presentation is to collect questions for people in other departments or divisions that you can't answer.

But that's rarely the case. Most of the time you're considered the expert when you're in front of the room.

The other thing that can happen is that people will ask questions that are not related to your presentation or are completely off the subject matter at hand.

You have three options here.

You can obviously answer the question, weave the question into your subject matter, or kindly suggest, "It's not something that we're really going to be discussing here today, but please feel free to check with me after my presentation is over."

What you decide to do in this case really depends on the question and the audience.

One last option would be to write down on a flip chart, questions that aren't currently being addressed or that you don't have the answer to (commonly referred to as a "parking lot").

I generally don't like this format, because it turns me into a "scribe" for the audience, which isn't a pretty site, and sometimes these things turn into a gripe session. People will start barking out comments instead of asking questions, and the whole thing becomes more therapeutic than productive.

But if handled correctly, a "parking lot" does not have to disrupt the flow of good Q & A. Sometimes when I do automotive or high-tech consulting, I essentially become a spokesperson for a particular manufacturer or company. They may require and the situation may demand that there be a "parking lot".

If I'm obligated to do one, and I inadvertently open up a can of worms in the process, I say to the participants, "Alright, I can see that there's a lot of passion about this, but let's stick to the things that we can control here in this class today. What do we have control over? Those are the things that we should focus on." This helps everyone stay on track.

It's been said that there is no such thing as a dumb question. Basically I agree, but there are exceptions.

I was recently on a cruise, and sure enough during one of the introductory meetings on the first day, one of the passengers asked the Cruise Director, "What happens to the ice carvings in the restaurant after they melt?" Now that's a dumb question!

What happens if the question is dumb or irrelevant?

First of all never embarrass an audience member under any circumstances. If a question is either dumb or has already been asked, use the opportunity to give a more detailed answer or rephrase the question to serve your own agenda in a different way.

You're clever enough to turn a dumb, irrelevant question, or one that's been heard before into something that will take you to new heights. Look at this as a chance to resell an idea or gain new customers, while being a seemingly compassionate presenter.

If you have a heckler or someone who is rude or interrupts, what should you do? Surprisingly, this doesn't happen as often as you might think.

Just like a dog or a shark, a sociopath bent on making you look bad can sense when you're afraid or struggling. This will only encourage him and then others into a feeding frenzy at your expense.

Mastery of your physical presentation skills will typically deal with anyone who wants to rock the boat. Most troublemakers test the waters early on and when they see that they can't rattle your cage they give up.

You can usually sense these individuals and I typically look them right in the eye early on to let them know how comfortable I feel around them.

This diffuses their desire to attack right up front, and it's smooth sailing almost all of the time from there. Generally, the audience is relieved.

If for some reason you get that bad apple who just insists on being obnoxious, handle it firmly but with style and grace, and get the audience on your side to help you manage this person. Here's what I mean.

Someone asks a negative question. Well, that's easily dealt with by rephrasing the question and not answering back to that individual.

Now the person insists on asking other questions and interrupts you. I'll give that individual one more question.

After two, if it happens again I'll say, "I'm glad that there's so much enthusiasm about this topic on your part, but let's allow some others to ask a few questions". That' s dealt with the problem effectively every time, and I've never had a problem.

If someone flat out heckles me (and that almost never happens), I'll gladly give that person the floor to ask a question. Then I'll rephrase, lock in the standard Q & A skills, and that takes care of that.

When you allow a heckler to be heard and you handle the situation confidently and smoothly, the problem is essentially over.

You certainly have the option to say to someone, "There's a great deal more involved with all of this and I'd be happy to discuss this with you afterwards." And then break visually to another audience member.

That tells the audience that you're not being defensive and that there is a time concern here for everyone. It also indicates that you'd like to give others a chance.

If you have to leave, don't suddenly say, "Well I've got to go now. See you later."

Rewind to two questions back and say something like, "I've got another engagement that I need to get to, but I do have time for two more questions".

Two is the perfect number. It's more than one, it's a handful, but it allows you the time to get away. They may have wanted more time, but two more questions is considered to be reasonable.

The last thing I leave my students with regarding Q & A, are two trump cards, just in case the questioning gets tough.

I don't give them this information right up front because then they'll start relying on these two safety valves before they learn some of the other Q & A basics.

The first one is what I term the great neutralizer.

When rephrasing a question under fire it's sometimes difficult to think of a positive or neutral rephrase. So I introduce the "What about *(insert neutralized subject matter)*?" model. This will typically neutralize every question. And we test it in class so participants see how it works.

So if someone asks, "Why did you shut down the factory?" the rephrase would be, "So, what about the factory status?"

Another example might be "Hasn't this drug killed some people already?" The rephrase, " What about the track record of this drug?"

"What about *(insert neutralized subject matter)*?" will just about neutralize every tough question out there. Give it your own test.

The last trump card is only for absolute emergencies and must be used sparingly.

What if someone stuns you with a very tough question? It's unexpected and you are caught off guard, but want to regain your composure immediately.

You may ask that person to repeat the question, pretending you didn't hear it or understand it.

THIS IS A SAFETY VALVE ONLY because, keep in mind, the questioner now has the opportunity to drag you through the mud one more time and repeat his negative question or become even more hostile.

The other challenge is that if you use this technique too often, the audience will think that you're either hard of hearing or stupid.

You may want to consider saying, "I think I understand the question, but can you put it another way." That sounds better than, "Can you repeat the question", and it may take some of the sting out of it.

As a final note, make a list of difficult questions that your audience may ask you. Ask co-workers to come up with an inventory of the toughest questions out there.

Also ask for appropriate responses, send out e-mails, and use electronic bulletin boards to ask for the toughest questions along with the best possible answers and responses.

If you anticipate these questions and are already familiar with them, you won't become as shell-shocked when you get nailed in the real world.

Many companies I consult with have incorporated this idea from Kahrs Communication Concepts very effectively. Many have also set up Q & A practice sessions where employees will rehearse rephrasing, answering, and all of the challenges discussed in this section.

It's a wonderful idea and it will make you feel more comfortable when traveling into the uncharted waters of Q & A!

Part Seven

Media Relations

Close-ups

Because there are so many transferable skills from presentation skills to media skills, I've included a section in this book to help you, just in case you're ever thrown into such an environment.

Presentation skills and media skills have many similarities, but there are some extremely important differences to consider as well.

The first thing to remember is that there will be a lot of camera close-ups!

What that basically means is that everything you do physically is amplified. One frown, one tear, one off color remark, and it's watched by millions around the world. Even someone with a satellite dish in Eastern Nepal, is catching your mistake or angry snarl on CNN.

The other thing is that everything in media is sound bite driven. It's the little catch phrases like "Can't we all get along?" "If it doesn't fit, you must acquit" that make the headlines.

The good news is that you can take advantage of this medium by having a series of sound bites tucked away ready to deliver during an interview. In fact, I highly recommend that you prepare many sound bites and that you reread the section on Q & A rephrasing before ever meeting with a journalist on camera.

The bad news is that your longwinded answers or responses may be taken out of context and turned into a sound bite that doesn't really represent your point of view and shows you in a negative light.

It's an important point to know, and just substantiates how crucial it is to never appear negative or angry on camera, even if you truly feel you have the right to be that way.

An edited clip of you being angry or upset can be shown to TV audiences over and over again. Suddenly you are perceived as an angry person.

Being firm, or being serious can certainly be effective. Your words may denounce, deny, or attack, but never lose your composure or appear out of control.

The other challenge, especially with TV, is that there never is enough time to say what you really want to say.

Often times you are competing with other speakers and commercial time. And most journalists aren't at a loss for words. That's why they do what they do. Have you ever seen longtime journalist Sam Donaldson sit quiet for long?

The craftiest media presenters are able to get their agenda out, no matter what is asked or said about them, and they are able to do it in a positive way. It's really an art to be able to accomplish this and it's always fascinating to watch a polished politician pull this off.

I am reminded of the '88 election when Senator Lloyd Benson, a seasoned politician, and Dan Quayle were debating as vice-presidential candidates. Quayle compared himself with John Kennedy, desperately trying to build his own credibility.

Benson came back with his famous one-liner. "I knew John Kennedy. John Kennedy was my friend. You're no John Kennedy." It was the ultimate put-down.

Can you seriously respond to allegations? Can you appear passionate about something? Yes, but don't appear nervous, edgy, or angry. It will only hurt you in the long run. I've seen it happen too many times.

Business people are notorious for not coming off with the right amount of appeal on camera. They seem boring, stiff, and lacking in enthusiasm.

A couple of things about on camera interviews.

Remember to check out your surroundings ahead of time. It can be rather unsettling being thrown into a TV studio with the bright lights and cables everywhere if you're not used to it. Take it all in and get used to this environment.

It's ideal if you can have a remote interview at your house. These types of interviews are gaining in popularity all of the time, and it's a place where most of us probably feel most comfortable.

You'll want to look at the interviewer.

Many make the mistake of looking at the camera and then back at the interviewer or they sometimes quite frankly have no idea where to look. Always lock eyes with the interviewer unless told to do otherwise.

Remote interviews are becoming more and more popular. Nightline has been doing remote interviews for years, getting folks from various parts of the country to square off in debate as Ted Koppel moderates.

Many sports shows like Monday Night Football will have interviews with certain players at half time as they sit comfortably at home.

When doing remote interviews the camera should now become your main focus. Treat the camera like a person, although that's hard to visualize. Don't be tempted to look at the other TV monitors in the room showing the individual asking you questions.

Look directly into the "live" camera and always remember that people will be seeing your image even when you're listening to the journalist asking a question. Always act as if you're being watched and stay focused on the camera until the stage manager says that the interview is over.

If you're wearing an ear piece, try it on ahead of time, get comfortable with it, and make sure it fits. Ask the ground crew if you can test it first and make sure that the sound levels are to your liking. You don't want the sound levels to blast your head off while you're on TV.

Sometimes the ear piece will either go dead or fall out while someone is interviewing you or while you are talking. Don't panic!

If either happens, simply go ahead with an answer that you like. You could say for example, "Barbara, my ear piece seems to be malfunctioning but I'd like to add…" After you're through with your response, you can say, "I'm sorry Ted, my ear piece just went out on me, can you repeat that question again."

The beauty here is that the station will cut to commercial or think of something else to do if your answer is too long, but the pressure will be on them.

You have the floor and the audience knows that it's not your fault. As long as you're giving a nice upbeat answer with a possible rephrase like, "So am I qualified to do this job. You bet! The reason is…I mentioned earlier that…Thanks for your question and it's important for everyone to know…"

That's why it's so important to have little nuggets and sound bites tucked away and rehearsed in advance.

If your ear piece pops out, slowly put it back in your ear. I say slowly, because you're probably a little nervous and any sudden or quick movement may cause further headaches that you don't need.

Sit up in your chair, don't slouch back and try to hide. Use your hands freely and use the interviewer's first name.

Most importantly, smile early on and often to let the audience know how comfortable and happy you are to be there.

Unusual or sudden movements are out. Gestures are fine, but most audience members won't see them on camera, that's why facial expressions and voice inflection become increasingly important. That open friendly face with the eyebrows raised is a nice image for camera close-ups.

After the interview is over, don't bolt out of the chair or start to remove your microphone or your ear piece. Let the technicians worry about all of that and don't get up until you're told because you don't want the audience to think that you're nervous or eager to leave.

For all you know the cameras are still rolling while the moderator raps up the session.

Always consider yourself to be on camera, even if your interviewer is speaking with someone else. The studio operators may pan over to you, switch to a different camera or angle, and you could be on camera and not even know it.

If you happen to be picking your nose, the whole world will see. You are on, until the stage manager tells you the taping or session is over.

Verbal skills during TV interviews are again different because there is a limited amount of time. Never forget that. You must seize the opportunity to make your point before the program is finished.

If a reporter begins a negative attack and continues to role on with no end in sight, don't wait for him to finish.

For example if a reporter starts in, "We understand that this is not the first time an individual has complained about the side affects of this damaging pharmaceutical, in fact last week someone mentioned that..." You have to jump in at this point with something like, "I'd like to address that by saying..." or "As you know this has come to our attention and I'd like to respond immediately..."

When you are giving your answer make sure you finish completely. If you get interrupted say something like, "Just a moment Jill, I would like to address this important issue" or "There's a lot to say about all of this, Bob, but please let me finish this important point". Always remember to smile because you don't want to appear defensive or pushy.

If a question catches you off guard, buy yourself some time to think by saying, "Let's consider that for a moment..." or "So let me see if I understand you correctly..." Those precious few seconds will allow you to work wonders and allow you to process some more answers.

If you get a negative question, remember that you learned how to rephrase and neutralize that negative question. This is pure gold, especially relative to media skills. Being able to rephrase effectively will help you deal with any tough situation.

Politicians often not only rephrase questions, they just change them to serve their own agenda so that they can get out the information that they feel is important in the short period of time they have. In one way or another, they see to it that their ideas come across, regardless of what anyone else has to say.

It's extremely important not to repeat negative words or phrases. By repeating negativity you're almost admitting guilt. Rephrase or deny negativity, "I wouldn't say that at all…I believe that the issue is…"

Sometimes reporters will ask several questions at a time (2-3). It is not your responsibility to remember them all.

Take the one that you like best and run with it. Make your point and if you can weave the other question in there to your advantage, go for it. Otherwise the onus is on the reporter to ask you the remaining questions. That's what they get paid to do.

Occasionally reporters will force you to choose the answer to a closed-ended question when that's not really fair to you. "So will this decision help the patient or the company?" Resist picking one or the other. Your response might be, "The wonderful thing is that it'll really help both, here's why…"

Other times, reporters will ask hypothetical questions to get you to talk or speculate about something. If that's what you'd like to do, fine, but it can be risky to speculate, and who knows where and when that tape may come back to haunt you. You do have options here.

You can for example kindly avoid speculations by suggesting, "You know, Stephanie, it's fun for all of us to speculate, but I'd prefer to stick to the facts, and the facts are…" and then perhaps you can drive home your agenda again.

Another technique frequently used by TV journalists is silence. The thinking here, is that you will reveal more or keep talking if the reporter remains quiet. Mike Wallace from 60 Minutes is masterful at doing this. It's amazing how well this works most of the time for many reporters.

When you're done talking, stop. The reporter will eventually have to jump back in because too much dead silence on TV is deadly for ratings.

Your other option is to simply take that silence and address another significant issue. "You know John, you've got me thinking about another point that's important for me to share with you and your audience…"

If you start taking over the interview and promoting your own agenda every time the reporter uses silent tactics, the problem will take care of itself.

More than ever, journalists want to dig deeper and get extremely personal with interviewees about income, past behavior, sexual allegations. This sells.

If it is personal, you always have the right to politely refuse. "As I've stated before, Ann, these are personal issues that I don't think are important. However, I would like to talk about something that's important to all of us…" or "This is personal information, Jerry, and I'd prefer not to discuss this in public, but let's talk about what's at stake here…"

Notice in all of these examples how we tie back to what we want to discuss.

You'll definitely want to rehearse and practice for the TV interview. Most important is that you fully understand your viewpoint. What is it? How does it impact the people watching? How will you convince us that it's the right thing to do?

Can you give us your point of view in a sound bite (10-20 seconds)? Can you support your viewpoint in 10-20 seconds? Practice it with your colleagues. Have your co-workers ask you tough questions. Rehearse rephrasing and, practice giving back great answers that tie back to your ideas.

Just like using evidence to support your presentation, don't hesitate to use the various forms of evidence to support any ideas that you may be promoting here. But remember, this is TV, make it short, sweet, and to the point.

Also think in terms of what appeals to the viewing audience. Would they prefer statistics or an analogy? A true story or an anecdote? Can you describe something so that we can visualize it? How long will it take?

Unless you're hosting a show on fly-fishing, make sure that you dress conservatively for TV. Remember, this is an image of you being projected to thousands possibly millions of people. Dress appropriately for the camera.

White does not show up well on camera. Grays, pastels, and light blues are ideal for TV. Avoid busy patterns and flashy clothes or shiny jewelry that may distract from your message.

Epilogue

Are great speakers made or are they born? Well, yes and no.

I'd be out of business if great speakers were born. Obviously, you can learn how to become a highly competent presenter.

In my ten years of training, I have seen incredible turn arounds in short periods of time. I've seen people who are terrified and have no apparent natural ability to speak, in fact become great presenters who are admired and respected.

On the other hand, I have seen some people who have lots of natural ability, resist the chance to change and as a consequence leave their abilities at an average level. But that's a matter of choice.

Roughly speaking, 80% of my students who spend at least one day with me (two is ideal) make dramatic improvements and I mean dramatic. The other 19% make significant changes, and invariably there are about 1%, who just, for whatever reason, don't get it.

That's not bad when considering public speaking is the number one fear that people have.

Since this is a comprehensive book I do need to mention that every once in a great while, a student of mine possesses, what I call, an "x factor".

This individual breaks every rule in the book. They don't make eye contact, they pace all over the place, and they use the same awkward gestures over and over again. They use non-words constantly and prepare visuals that don't work. In fact, we're lucky if they've prepared anything at all.

But all of this doesn't matter, the audience loves this presenter and they can do anything, and it looks good. This individual can get away with breaking every guideline ever created by consultants, speakers, or trainers.

I meet someone like this about once a year. And when I do, I point out a few things that we can learn from that person, namely that they typically have a very high energy level and they generally are very sincere. They also have a sense of humor and a sense of who they are.

But let's face it, most of us aren't that one in a million. Most of us can learn to be much better presenters and most of us can make dramatic improvements that will make sure our message gets heard and that our career stays on track.

I hope this book has been helpful to you and I hope you have as much fun using these skills as I did writing this book for you. Please let me know your thoughts and as always, please stay in touch and remember, making a mistake or two in front of people will never be fatal. Just hang in there and you'll get through.

There's the old show business adage "never let 'em see you sweat". And remember, the audience doesn't know that you're nervous. You know the presentation better than anyone does else does. You are now armed with an arsenal of methods and techniques that will always make you look good.

Use that nervous energy productively to energize your presentation. Enjoy yourself and your joy will become contagious. Good luck!

Part Eight (Bonus Section)

*An Introduction to the
"Consultative Tool Box Technique"*

Preface

Whether it's been working with new or existing clients, promoting my own communication skills firm, or working for Fortune 500 companies, I've been involved in sales in one form or another for over 20 years.

During the later half of my training career, I have done a lot of consulting in the automotive field. What I've noticed is that things have changed dramatically in the car business, and the industry as a whole has gone through a major metamorphosis.

More than ever, young and old come into car dealerships armed with manufacturer invoice information, specifications, and comparisons on a vehicle before they even look at a new one or walk onto the showroom floor.

We joke in the car business, which is a very traditional industry, that sometimes these customers know more than we do. Many times that's true.

But a remarkable thing has happened. The car business, which has roots all the way back to the old horse-trading days, has changed and adjusted to the new customer and successfully embraced a new way of doing business.

Having consulted with numerous industries from high-tech, to pharmaceuticals, from telecommunications to investment banking; I believe that selling comes down to some basic principles regardless of the product.

Reverence for the buyer, client, or customer must be inherent in everything we do. Each individual needs to be treated with respect, dignity, and sincere understanding. Trickery, manipulation, or deception will only serve to hurt any sales process in the long run. Maintaining integrity and having a true interest in whoever we deal with is paramount to our success, and the ultimate satisfaction of who we do business with.

I've done seminars for companies that manufacture everything from penile implants to RV portable toilets, and I've found that certain sales principles and ideas transcend the product or service itself, and even the subject of sales. Sometimes selling is more about psychology and human relations than anything else.

Many sales training seminars and books that I've studied suggest that there is a sales process. Different companies have different names for it, but it's basically a "steps to the sale" merry-go-round or wheel that is highlighted with various bold-faced words and acronyms that represent different corporate visions or ideals.

What has always amazed me is how many companies create a sales process, based on what they think happens or based on how they believe things should go.

The reality is that the sales process almost never goes the way we think it's supposed to go. If you've been selling for any length of time, you will know exactly what I'm talking about.

Our clients don't always conform to the order that we've created for them to follow. One customer may go right to step 5, then back to step 3, and perhaps wants to start all over again. But that's O.K., because that's what that particular customer wants to do.

The problem here for us is that there is no sales process that occurs the same way every time. The fact that we try to force customers into a certain process to begin with is in my opinion problematic.

Some customers require reassurance, third party accolades, or a host of other important affirmations. Every customer is different and every customer has different needs.

Many customers want to be on their way once they've decided to purchase a product or service. But some "old school" practices suggest that we burden these customers with the entire sales process, whether they like it or not.

Furthermore, with the advent of e-commerce, e-business, and the Internet, old sales models don't work anymore. The "old school" ways are passe. People are smarter, more informed, and less tolerant of worn sales practices than ever before.

If someone doesn't like a sales process, they can just shop on-line and get a product delivered to their house. Many would prefer this anyway.

In all my years of sales and sales training there are two things I know about sales for sure. One, someone has a product or service to sell. Number two, if enough people don't buy this product or service the company selling this product or service will go out of business.

That's basic and that's raw, but that's what it all boils down to in very rough terms. We have to figure out the best way to get our product/service to as many people as possible, as efficiently as possible.

Because most people don't want to be "sold" anymore and because no sales cycle is exactly the same every time, I believe the best approach is to treat every customer individually and consult with him, communicate with her, and lead them ultimately where he or she wants to go.

Now of course, that's easier said than done. I'm not being naïve, but it's simply a better way over the long haul.

Traditional sales models also have steps, levels, and even more acronyms to remember to ultimately close the sale. The challenge here is that it's hard to remember so many different steps, rules, and examples when you are in the middle of a presentation, discussion, or an onslaught of objections.

If a potential customer has an objection over a solution you just came up with, are you thinking to yourself, "Gee, where am I in the sales process? Step 4? Step 7? What should I do now? Maybe I'll go through the 'Steps to the Sale' again?"

The point is you're in the middle of a negotiation and you're stuck. Thinking about acronyms or fancy phrases won't help. You need some real help. Hopefully that's where this book will be of assistance.

All of the dialogue skills needed to deal with customers and clients in a consultative fashion are basically already in existence. But most of these skills, don't come from business, they come from psychology.

What I will attempt to do in this section of the book is distill the best thinking from psychology and sales, and present these dialogue skills to you.

I also want to create an arsenal of these basic dialogue skills and create for you what is know as the "Toolbox". These words and phrases contained in the "Toolbox" are not complicated; in fact you use them every day. Some of them will have names and perhaps I'll introduce an acronym.

This will result in a simplification of the sales process and in greater flexibility.

And since this process will be client and customer driven, there is no particular order or pattern you have to follow.

Because there is no rigid sequence, the whole method becomes user-friendly for you and less threatening for the client. It is consultative.

These basic selling skills, psychological principles, and the notion that the only sales process that works consistently is the one driven by the customer is what I call the "Consultative Toolbox Technique."

Like with a toolbox, I'm going to suggest that you only use the tools when you need them. In other words, if you need to nail something down, use a hammer, if you need to tighten a screw, you need to use a screwdriver, and so forth.

The point here is that you only use what you need when you need it. And it is all driven by what the client, customer, or person wants, not what you want. In a nutshell, I will give you all of the basic elements of consultative selling skills and I will give them to you in user-friendly terms that are easy to learn and natural to use.

What's more, these skills that you'll learn can be applied to all aspects of business and life, since we're basically talking psychology here. So, whether you're interviewing for a job, conducting the interview, buying a car, selling a house, or working something out with your spouse, these dialogue skills can be universally applied to all human interactions.

On the business communication side, all of these skills can be applied to hiring and managing, telephone and writing skills, and even presentation and media skills. They transcend all boundaries of business, and can be incorporated by web-based businesses as well.

Keep in mind that these skills are completely interchangeable and can be used over and over again, in all types of different situations. They are designed to seem natural and conversational because I believe no one wants to be sold or manipulated. These words and phrases will seem inherent because for the most part, you use them every day.

By learning to listen and to ask the right questions, you will be able to help the customer make logical decisions and choices. The "Consultative Toolbox Technique" will help you develop productive conversations rather than creating a forced dialogue.

It's important to note that these techniques that I'm about to share with you are not magic. Your sales volume will not automatically double in 2 days, you will not see exponential growth in your company's stock within one week. But hopefully your batting average will increase.

The analogy of baseball, still officially the nation's past time, is great to use here.

Let's compare two baseball players who are perfect defensive players, outfielders. They don't make any mistakes defensively; they are Golden Glove recipients.

Well there is a slight difference between these two guys. One of them gets 2 hits out of every ten at bats (.200 hitter) and the other one gets 3 hits out of every ten at bats (.300 hitter).

I make the point in my seminars that a .200 hitter doesn't last long in the major leagues and is ultimately shipped out to a farm team in a smaller city for an average salary of about $25,000.00. I've checked it out personally, and many players actually make even less than that.

Now, the .300 hitter will make a minimum of about 3 million a year, and that's at the low end. Is it because he's almost three million times better than his friend, who just got shipped down to the minors? Of course not, it's because he's one more time out of ten better; that's all. That little bit makes a big difference.

In today's business world, golf is by in large the most popular sport around. The same logic can be applied to golf.

What separates the world's number 1 player from the world's 150th ranked player is typically just under one stroke per round of golf. That's simply amazing, and this little difference is worth several million dollars in prize money, not to mention all of the endorsements!

In this same way, if you incorporate these new skills that I'll share with you, you may in fact hit one more ball out of ten or possibly reduce your round by a stroke or two; and that, I hope, will make a big difference in all of your relationships.

Who Is This About Anyway?

Back in the early nineties when I was still relatively new to sales training, I co-facilitated a seminar in Pennsylvania with another instructor. During the first day of training we had heated debates with participants about what the best sales approach was.

My well-seasoned partner exclaimed, "Treat people the way you want to be treated!"

"Sounds reasonable," I thought to myself, but suddenly one of the participants became furious and attacked my co-facilitator, "You've got it all wrong, you've got to treat people the way they want to be treated, not the way you want to be treated."

My partner, an experienced and skilled facilitator, tried to save face, but somehow everyone in the room instinctively knew that our irate participant was right on the money.

We've all heard about the Golden Rule: "Do unto others as you would have them do unto you." Not bad, but we need to do better than that. How about the Platinum Rule: "Treat people the way they want to be treated." That's even better.

The whole point is that it's about the other person, the customer, or the client. It is not about you. O.K., perhaps that sounds too easy, too simple, and maybe you're thinking, "Yea, I know that."

Be honest with yourself, though! Did you really listen to the last person that you spoke with, either face to face or on the phone? Did you really care or show empathy by your actions? Did you jump to conclusions during your last appointment with one of your customers? Did you truly know what they needed, or could you have perhaps probed a little more or been a little more patient?

As businesspeople, many of us get too focused on our agenda, in fact, so focused that sometimes we don't care what our customer wants. We just know that we want to sell or that we need to close the deal.

Let's slow down for a moment and go back to the very beginning.

Opening the Dialogue

"A gossip talks about others, a bore talks about himself, a brilliant conversationalist talks about you."

—*Anonymous*

When you meet with a customer, especially if it's a first meeting or a cold call, what should you say first? It's always a dilemma.

It's a precarious position to be in because you don't know. And because we don't know, many of us just start rambling. If we're salespeople, that's what we do. We start talking.

Buyers know this about us, and they love it because they just sit back and start listening to us go on and on.

It's fun for them because they'll have no idea what we'll be talking about or where we'll be going. Some of us start talking about sports, others about the stock market, maybe even the weather.

But it's a risky approach because who knows what our customers are really thinking? Are they sizing us up? Are they trying to gain an edge in the negotiation process? Do they even like sports, who knows? It's literally a crapshoot for us…but there's hope!

Take the pressure off of yourself by opening the dialogue with what I call an OPIner.

O-*Open* the dialogue with a salutation, a greeting.

P-Give the customer a *preparation* statement.

I-*Invite* the customer to speak.

So instead of guessing about what to talk about, say something like, "Hi, thanks for agreeing to meet with me, I certainly have some things I can share with you, but please tell me about what's going on."

Interesting approach. I am now telling the client that I'd be happy to start talking but that, perhaps, he'd like to say a few words first, in fact I'm encouraging it.

This also reduces the need for me to be psychic. After all, it's very well possible that I may not know what is on the mind of the client.

It gets the meeting off on the right foot and allows the customer to direct the conversation. In this way, you don't have to guess whether or not this person is interested in sports, other activities, or perhaps wants to get right down to business.

Notice also how open-ended and casual the Invitation part of the OPIner is: "…tell me about what's going on."

Obviously it can be more formal and/or more directed towards a specific area: "…how was your last quarter and what's the status of your new production facility?" Moreover, you can have many variations here and obviously design your own OPIner.

Here's another example: "It's great to see you again, we have some new things I'd like to show you, but tell me, how's business?"

Again, *O*pen, *P*reparation, *I*nvitation. It's all there.

When you understand this concept you won't even need to remember any words. You can create them off the top of your head. That's much more conversational anyhow.

It's important to note that the OPIner does not contain the word *problem* or *needs*. For example: "It's great to see you again, we have some new things I'd like to show you, but tell me about your *problems* (*needs*)."

This is chancy because you are implying that your customer has a problem or has needs. That may be a little too forceful or presumptuous (especially during a first meeting) and the client may be thinking to himself, "No I don't have problems, but you certainly do right now." So, be careful!

Some of my students correctly point out that an OPIner doesn't always work and that often times a customer will throw it back in your lap. I have to agree.

Amazingly though, it does work over 50% (closer to 85%) of the time, based on my experience and the experience of my clients. Buyers love to feel in control and to talk about themselves. When given the chance to talk about themselves, very few people can resist.

If someone does throw it back in your lap, then you can go on with your presentation, because you've certainly tried to encourage him or her to speak. As you will learn when you read on, there are also other ways to draw people out.

The beauty of the OPIner is that it sets the tone for the entire meeting and will also help you stay on track with your client.

Perhaps your client wants to talk about something completely different today. Maybe he or she had a meeting this morning, just before you walked in that completely changes everything relative to the direction you had in mind. Isn't that something you'd like to know before you get into your canned pitch?

If they want a product that they don't know you have, they may have to buy it from someone else because you're so focused on selling them something they don't need.

We can all think of a time that that's happened to us.

Don't run off of a plank at full speed. Let the customer lead you down the right path.

Because the OPIner typically occurs at the very beginning, it's a crucial component of the "Consultative Toolbox Technique". It's probably the only skill that you will learn that will consistently be used during a particular sequence in the dialogue; the beginning.

Active Listening

"Why do you have two ears but just one mouth?"

Your Mother

At the swap meet when I was waiting for my license plate frame for "thetrainer4u.com" (now my official .com address) to be completed, I decided to walk around and check out the booths in the area.

It was right after the holiday season, so it was a slow day and lots of the booths that had extensive sound systems, trinkets, and anything to arouse curiosity, seemed empty.

However, this one little booth had all of the action, so I thought I'd take a look to see what all of the fuss was about.

So, the smallest booth at the weekend swap meet in Southern California has the most action. Why?

Well the booth offered an instant family tree research service. In other words, you could look up your family name in a master book and then find out the history of your family and the origins of your family (last) name.

There was a long line in front of the one computer terminal that had additional information about your family's history.

So why was this the busiest place at the entire swap meet? Because people like to hear and find out about themselves. Everyone's favorite subject is himself or herself.

If you understand this and act accordingly by listening actively, I believe it'll make a difference not only in your business life, but in your personal life as well. Take a genuine interest in other people and learn from them. It can only help.

Do you know someone, maybe even someone you love, who talks too much? Perhaps we are all somewhat guilty of doing this. Interestingly enough, some of the most successful people that I've met, speak very little. They listen.

But how can you accomplish this? What does active listening really require and how do you keep the conversation going?

This all reminds me of the time that I was in high school and I was in my afternoon Geometry class.

Typically after lunch, all students were tired, including myself. The teacher Mr. Davis started talking about theorems, which put all of us further to sleep. However, I did not want to get called on, so I made eye contact with my teacher and bobbed my head up and down, trying to indicate that I was listening.

Truthfully, I was not listening, but rather daydreaming.

Unfortunately, Mr. Davis looked deep into my eyes after about ten minutes and said to me, "Well Till, you seem to understand what I am talking about. Could you please come up here and explain this theorem to the rest of the class?"

I was caught off guard, but quickly recovered by asking to be excused to go to the bathroom. I had not listened to a word he had said.

So the lesson here is that you can only fake active listening up to a certain point. To let your clients, employees, friends know that you're truly listening, you must incorporate one basic skill set and probably combine that skill set with several others to make sure that you keep the conversation going.

What are the mechanics of active listening? Be kind, rewind, or as I like to say, Replay.

To make sure that you're really staying on track, Replay or playback what you just heard, using a lead in phrase like: "So what I hear you saying is…" "Let me make sure I've got this…" "To make sure I understand you correctly…" Then of course you would insert what you think you just heard.

Notice that I don't say, "So what *you're* saying is…" The reason is simple. I want to put the onus on me if I misinterpreted what the client said. Therefore, it's better to say, "So what *I hear* you saying is…" This way the client can always save face.

Replaying the information does not mean that you agree with what the client is saying, but it does indicate that you are listening.

After playing back the information, the dialogue typically advances because the client will either agree, disagree, or change your Replayed message. Either way, you're getting more information and the customer sees you as a good listener. This client may be thinking, "He's listening to what I have to say. He's pretty smart."

Amazingly and surprisingly, most salespeople don't do this.

The Replay technique also helps you buy some time to think. That's important sometimes during a heated discussion. We could all use a few extra moments now and then to consider our next course of action.

If a customer is leaning forward and nodding his head in agreement with what you are repeating back to them, that's a good thing. It builds rapport, and it also gives you time to respond appropriately.

Replaying is also an excellent way to summarize information to make sure that you are not leaving out any important details.

Finding Out More

"Better to let them think you are a fool, than to open your mouth and have it confirmed"

—*Anonymous*

To find out more information we need to Explore.

Incidentally, the techniques of Replaying and Exploring work hand in hand and can be dropped into dialogue anywhere and as often as needed, during the sales process. These two skills sets are probably the most important that you will learn in this section and can greatly impact the way you do business.

By Exploring we are attempting to dig below the surface and find out more information about our client. These Exploring tools are often times referred to as clarifiers or probes.

No matter what you call them, they help us get the client to open up and talk.

Here are some examples:

"Tell me more."

"Why do you say that?"

"In what way?"

"How so?"

"And?"

"Go on."

"What else should I know?"

"Is there anything else I should know?"

These open-ended probes allow the customer to speak freely and these clarifiers also encourage longer, more detailed answers. That's good for us because we're getting smarter when our customers talk more.

Careful that you use the last two Exploring tools listed sparingly and not at the beginning of your exploratory mission, because if you ask, "What else should I know?" right up front and there isn't anything else. You're done.

Also, "Is there anything else I should know" is what I refer to as the "dust-buster". Use that as a last resort when you've exhausted all of the other tools. It's a great way to check and see if there are any crumbs being left on the table.

Often times these leftover crumbs turn into gold nuggets if we just take the time to Explore one last time.

When using the Exploring method make sure that you are conversational. If you hit a client with, "Why did you say that?" and it's an angry snarl, it won't come across the right way.

There's a saying in the German language, "Der Ton macht die Musik". "The tone makes the music." Make sure you use the correct tone with your customers.

One way to soften your tone and become more conversational is to use an acknowledgement before a clarifier. For example:

"*I'm curious*, why do you ask?"

"*Really*, how so?"

An acknowledgement by itself can become a probe if used correctly with the right inflection:

"Oh, really?"

"Oh?"

Just remember to pause. And wait for the client to speak.

Confucius once said, "When in doubt, silence is the best companion." I agree.

Remember that we need to pause when using all of these skills. Whether you are Replaying or Exploring, it's crucial. Don't finish someone's thought, and don't try to guess what his response is going to be. That can be disastrous.

After you Replay or after you Explore, hesitate, count to three; pause.

Let your customer speak and give her the time to respond. Otherwise you run the risk of getting back on the plank and running right off.

Specifiers are also Exploring tools that you can use in the same way. They are called Specifiers because they are designed to give you specifics. Here are some examples of commonly used Specifiers:

"Tell me more about…"

"For example?"

"Such as?"

(Repeat Key Words)

If someone gives you a very broad answer like, "I don't like to do business that way." You may say, "For example?" An alternative would be to repeat the key words (which means echo back what you want to know more about). So you'd say, "Don't like to do business that way?"

Still another tool at your disposal, are Emoticons.

They are very similar to the clarifiers and probes we just learned, but with a different twist. They draw out emotion, hence Emoticons.

Consider that occasionally all these verbal tools can be so effective, a customer may share something very personal, revealing, or noteworthy with you. For example, "A lot is riding on this because this could mean a promotion." Or, "If we don't do something about this I'll lose my job."

In these two instances you are getting some very sensitive information. As always, you must be respectful of your clients' feelings. Instead of using a standard, "Tell me more," or "Why do you say that?" We may need to be a little bit more sensitive in our approach and say something like:

"How does this affect you personally?"

"I sense this means a lot to you?"

"This sounds real important. Please tell me more."

These are Emoticons.

What you've done here is adjusted the expression of your probe to match the sensitivity of the information that has just been shared with you.

It's a minor adjustment perhaps, but all of these little things will start adding up.

Replaying and Exploring allow you to relinquish control. Don't grab the steering wheel. Let the other person drive for a while and don't be a back seat driver.

These dialogue skills can be so powerful that I often get asked, "What happens if someone talks too much or you get off track?"

The solution here is simple, Replay and then redirect your probe. So, playback what you've heard from the client so far, and then try to lead the customer in a different direction.

If a client gets off on a tangent, kindly interrupt and suggest, "Let me make sure that I've got this straight. I hear you saying that…(Replay). Please, tell me more about: insert whatever direction that you would like this to go."

By Replaying you're suggesting that you're listening. By using a Specifier you are controlling which way you want the conversation to unfold from there.

I always tell my students that you do have one more alternative in handling a talkative individual, which is to say, "Tell me more, some other time." Of course I'm only kidding.

Psychologist or Private Eye?

While flying to Vancouver, Canada, to give a sales seminar, I noticed that the person next to me kept peeking over at my notes.

I was preparing some dialogue skills information for my upcoming class and my inquisitive neighbor inquired, "So are you going to the Psychology Convention?" I informed him otherwise and he responded, "Oh, I was just looking at your material and I thought for sure you were a fellow psychologist." Perhaps my curious traveling companion's hunch was correct.

When I say that these verbal skills are straight from psychology, I'm absolutely serious.

It needs to be noted, however, that psychologists are obviously highly skilled and educated professionals, and that their subject matter is far more complex than simply incorporating a few words or phrases with their patients.

But psychologists do, on occasion, ask their patients, "Tell me more about that" or "How do you feel about that?" They also may Replay important details to make sure that they are gathering the right information.

Just like psychologists try to unravel mysteries using dialogue skills, so do private investigators. Being in sales you sometimes feel like a private eye.

TV detective Columbo was brilliant at using the Replay/Explore method. He would always use great open probes and also listen by playing back information.

Of course the suspect always thought that they were in control because they were doing all of the talking, when in fact Columbo was getting smarter all of the time, while the suspects kept digging themselves deeper in a hole.

Columbo was smart and non-threatening in his approach. He never appeared controlling or domineering, but he always ended up getting what he wanted.

We could learn a lot from Columbo.

Often times I end the first day of my two-day sales and negotiating classes with the Columbo story and it's a great way to set up the homework assignment for that evening, and to generate some excitement for the next day.

I tell my class, "We've learned some interesting things today, and I promised you that there are many practical non-business applications to these dialogue skills."

"What I'd like you to do this evening is try Replaying/Exploring on some unsuspecting people. Perhaps your spouse, your kids, a friend, and of course you may try these skills on the phone. In fact, they may be easier to use on the phone because you can cheat and look at your notes."

"Seriously though, the goal is to try to get people to talk and open themselves up for as long as you can without them knowing what you're actually doing. In other words, be as conversational as possible but be inconspicuous, while getting that individual to reveal more information."

The class starts imagining the possibilities and the stage is set for the homework assignment. I remind them to use what has been referred to as Verbal judo or Tongue-Fu, and then they are off to try their new found dialogue skills.

Invariably, the stories the next morning, are funny and amazing, but more importantly the class starts to recognize the power of these verbal tools.

Of course, I want my participants to have fun, but the homework assignment also proves that the "Consultative Toolbox Technique" actually works.

The countless humorous stories continue the next day, as one man explains how his wife was surprised that he finally listened or cared, or vice versa. But the greatest story I've heard on the second day was from a father in Seattle who had used the skills when conversing with his teenage son.

The father explained that his son had come home from football practice and seemed dejected. The father indicated that he had tried a few Replays, restating the fact that his son had not had a good day.

He followed up and started to Explore with "Tell me more." "Why do you say that?"

After several minutes, the father discovered that the high school football coach had encouraged his son to take steroids, an incredible revelation.

The father almost became tearful, as he explained how he might have never found out about this had it not been for the class. The whole class was rather shaken up by all of this.

On a more humorous note, one time a participant did not comprehend that REPEAT KEY WORDS meant echoing back actual words that where being said to him. He explained that he had said, "REPEAT KEY WORDS" to several individuals and didn't understand why people just kept looking at him in a peculiar way when he did this.

Open-Ended Questions

Another component of Exploring or investigating (for you Columbo fans) is the use of open-ended questioning.

Interestingly enough most individuals, especially sales people, understand the definition of an open-ended question versus a closed-ended question. It's generally accepted that open-ended questions are more effective, especially at the beginning of any business dialogue.

In my classes, after definitions of open-ended versus closed-ended questions have been correctly established by the audience, I ask the class collectively to ask me a series of open-ended questions off the top of their heads in about 3-4 minutes time.

Invariably, even after clearly defining the difference between open versus closed-ended questions in class, less than 5% of the questions I get asked are actually open-ended. Rarely is it 10%.

The point is that few actually understand how to structure open-ended questions, even though they know the definition.

Closed-ended questions typically give you yes or no responses and short one-word, non-detailed answers. They can also set up a multiple-choice answer, asking whomever you ask to pick just one response.

Closed-ended questions typically start with:

"Can you…?"

"Are you…?"

"Will you…?"

"What kind…?"

"Which model…?"

"When will you…?"

"Have you…?"

"Do you…?"

"Did you…?"

"Have you…?"

"How much…?"

"Where will you…?"

"Who is…?"

"Would you…?"

Open-ended questions typically require more detailed answers and incite the flow of the conversation.

They typically start with:

"Tell me about…"

"How do you like…?"

"Why are you…?"

"What are you…?"

Sometimes a closed-ended question may get a detailed long response if the customer feels like talking anyway.

Conversely, an open-ended question does not guarantee a long detailed answer, and a client can certainly choose to play "hard to get" and not be very open, even if you do use this technique. Nothing is ever guaranteed.

For this reason don't forget to use the Replay/Explore method (including Specifiers and Emoticons) in tandem with good open-ended questions. Obviously you could use this technique to open up closed-ended questions as well.

Closed-ended questions make you work harder because you're always getting short answers back. The onus, therefore, constantly ends up being back on you to ask more questions.

So asking a long list of closed-ended questions ends up like being on an incredibly bad date. You do all the talking and the other person just gives you short responses. The spotlight keeps turning back to you, when it really should be on the other person you are conversing with. This can be exhausting.

It's uncomfortable, it's too much work, and it's so unnecessary to put yourself in that kind of a situation.

By and large, open-ended questions will give you more of what you need to know, to get the details and information that will get you to the sale.

For example, if you ask a closed-ended question, "Do you like this product?" You are essentially drawing a line in the sand and asking a customer to make a determination about whether they like it or not, forcing them to decide "yes" or "no".

The problem is, perhaps they like the product, just not the color. By forcing the decision you may not get that information.

However if you ask more openly, "How do you feel about this product?" You are not pushing for a "yes" or "no" and the customer may reveal to you that color is the only problem.

Also, when pressured into an immediate choice, most of us are inclined to say "no". After all, we've learned to just say "no" to strangers since we were young. Isn't it natural for most people to back off when we're not sure or being coerced? All of us are clients and customers, and most of us don't want to be pushed by anyone. That's normal.

When you feel challenged and unsure, you resort to "no". And "no" is a hard place to come back from when you are trying to sell somebody something.

The other problem with using closed-ended questions is that it's easier for people to lie to us. For example if I ask, "Are you looking to buy something today?" the response will probably immediately be "no" or "just looking". Customers typically don't want to indicate to us that they have a sense of urgency to buy.

On the other hand if I ask a more open-ended version of this question, "Tell me about your time frame." (This is technically a statement, but works great as an open-ended question). I may get a response like, "Well, I was considering doing something this week, maybe even today if I find the right color."

That serves us a lot better than, "no". That's an answer we can work with.

Finally, when asking closed-ended questions to close the sale we run the risk again of getting the proverbial "no" response.

For example if I ask, "So, can we do business today?", a typical response would be "No, I don't think so."

Ironically, this customer may be close to buying something from you, but because you've forced the issue, he or she may back off and walk away, after hours of hard work on your part.

Instead, why not try, "What do you think about this model?" That's a nice way of asking, "Is there anything else standing in the way of our doing business?" without putting any pressure on. This is essentially known as a trial close.

If the response is, "I love this model, it's great", then it may be appropriate to ask for the business directly with a closed-ended question. But always use an open-ended approach first before you become closed-ended.

If you are playing the numbers and percentages, it's simply safer that way. And remember we want to increase our batting average.

You can open up most closed-ended questions by changing the verbiage to "How do you *feel*...?" or "What do you *think*...?" In this way we ask a customer about his belief or opinion instead of forcing them to make a final decision.

The open-ended technique is a great way to trial close or to take the temperature of the customer, so to speak. It's to your advantage to take the temperature if the stakes are high. It's better than simply gauging whether the customer is hot or cold, or essentially alive or dead using the closed-ended method.

It's a more precise measure of where they are at, and it's an important component in ultimately closing the sale. It is also at the core of the whole consultative, non-threatening approach.

Handling Questions and Objections

When handling objections or questions there is really not one technique or strategy that is correct. But I do recommend that you incorporate all of the open-ended consultative techniques you have learned thus far to insure that you stay in the game!

Simply speaking, Replaying and Exploring will generally assist you when answering questions or fielding objections.

Let's examine questions first.

Questions from customers can often times be deceiving because there is an underlying meaning beneath the question you initially hear.

Let me share an example that I always use in the classroom of something that happened to me years ago. I was in the wine and spirits business for many years calling on food service, hotel, and restaurant chain headquarter offices.

The company that I worked for at the time had just introduced a new distilled spirit and they wanted me to get distribution of this particular brand in one of my accounts, a restaurant chain that had over 150 locations nationwide.

I made an appointment to see the buyer, who I had met on several occasions before.

I brought along samples and literature and a host of other goodies as I entered his office and began my pitch, talking about the growth in this particular category that I was presenting, the advertising we were doing to support this brand, etc., etc. It was the full-blown presentation.

At one point he stopped me in mid-sentence and said, "Would you be able to provide me with any type of trinkets, t-shirts, buttons, swizzle sticks, or banners to help our units promote this brand?" I lit up like a pinball machine!

I reached right for a bag that I had brought with me and proceeded to pull out every last promotional item that I had brought along. Not only did I have all of the items that he had mentioned. There were additional items as well, including tongue depressors. I was seemingly on my way to closing this deal, I thought!

As I pulled the last item out of my bag, the buyer spoke to me and said, "You know Till, these liquor companies that do this promotional stuff are really irresponsible. You hand out all of these items for free to us, and ultimately our customers. Then we get nailed for a law suit if something goes wrong and a customer drinks too much." I was bewildered.

I back-tracked and explained to the buyer that our company only did responsible promotions and that all of their managers, bartenders, waiters and waitresses would of course be trained on how to do responsible promotions.

Furthermore, I explained how my company had even developed a video-tape on how to conduct responsible promotions, knowing when to cut someone off, and offering cab rides, etc. I was able to save the sale and my buyer ordered the new product as well as promotional items for all locations.

But what I should have done is use a simple consultative strategy to have avoided the extra work that I had to go through.

If you get a question in business and it seems somewhat suspicious, simply dig a little deeper (Explore) to find out what the real question is before you respond. You may also want to offer a short answer back initially to avoid appearing "slippery".

Here's what I mean. Let's say a client asks me if I train CEOs and middle managers in my training business. My first inclination is to respond "Yes, I do" and then continue on with a long list of clients, middle managers, CEOs, etc. that I have worked with in this capacity.

But what if my client now says, "Well, I was actually looking to train our new employees." Now I'm running down the same wrong path as in the drink promotion example.

So let's go back to the previous training example, but use a more consultative approach.

Client: "Till, does your company train middle managers and CEOs?"

Answer/Explore: "Yes we've done a lot of that, but I'm curious why do you ask?"

Client: "Well, we are looking to train our new hires. Our management team is already up to speed."

Replay/Answer: "Oh, so what you're saying is that your management team has been trained already, but you are looking to train the new hires."

Client: "Exactly!"

Now I can respond to what the real issue is and avoid going down the wrong path or running off of the plank again.

When you get a question that is suspect, feel free to probe, but again you may want to give a short answer back from time to time, before you probe, as I did in the aforementioned example.

Sometimes a simple "yes" or "no" followed by a probe will suffice, but you may also give a short answer like:

"Well it really depends…"

"It's relative…"

This way you don't have to commit to a "yes" or "no" before you explore further.

If you suspect an underlying meaning: Answer/Explore & Replay/Answer as many times as you need to get to the real core of the issue. Tough questions like, "Do you do business with ABC Company?" may require that you keep digging.

Do they want to know if you are credible and doing business with other legitimate customers or will they be upset if they know you are doing business with a competitor? You won't know until you do some additional research. Don't take a chance and guess.

On a personal note, if someone asks you what you are doing Friday night, it could be because they want you to help them move or because they have an extra free ticket, front row center, to the hottest show in town.

If you respond that you've got nothing to do Friday night, be prepared to move some boxes.

Objections can essentially be handled the same way.

Let's say you get the classic objection, "You're too expensive."

Replay/Explore: "So you think we're too expensive. Why do you say that?"

Client: "Well, is that the best you can do?"

Replay/Explore: "You want to make sure that's the best deal? Tell me more."

Client: "I just want to make sure that I get a quantity discount and that you have credit terms, etc."

Apparently, this client really wants to know about credit terms, and quantity discounts. This is certainly different than simply wanting a lower price.

But many salespeople will react immediately and offer the lower price before even exploring what the real issue is, instantly reducing the size of their commission.

Consider also that many times the age-old objection of "You're too expensive", may be a ploy to get you to lower your price.

Because it works so often with salespeople, buyers routinely employ this technique. Why not? They've got nothing to lose.

The price objection could also be a stall, because the customer is either too busy or doesn't want to deal with you at the moment. But you'll never know for sure unless you investigate; Replay/Explore.

Flying blind or skeet shooting in the dark lowers your batting average. Get the information that you need to proceed the best way possible for both you and the client.

Once you have the objection down to the lowest common denominator after Replaying/Exploring, ask the client, "Is there anything else?"

The reason we dust-bust here with "anything else" is because it lets us know if there are any other objections outstanding.

It's important to get everything out on the table before we proceed any further, and if there are more objections Replay/Explore until you're down to the lowest common denominator again and the last objection.

If the client response is, "No, there's nothing else". Then it's time to move on.

At this point I usually indicate to my classes that we are literally being consultants and that we are being paid to give consultations, just like a doctor or lawyer. If a doctor or lawyer doesn't do a proper consultation for you, people term that malpractice.

Don't perform malpractice on your clients and customers.

Recommending/Proposing

If we've performed a proper consultation by using the OPIner, Replaying, Exploring, and using these skills to answer questions and objections. It's likely that sooner or later we will need to make our recommendation or proposal to that client.

You may have to come back another time to propose because your initial meetings have only been exploratory. However, whether or not you present your suggestions right then and there during your initial meeting, or come back at a later time, it should be done the correct way.

Exude confidence in your proposal/recommendation!

A great way to start off a proposal would be, "Based on what you've told me, here's what you should consider…" That's effective because it's based on what they told you, as opposed to, "Let me tell you what I think you need…" That's not a very consultative approach.

After you make your proposal or recommendation it's nice to use value statements to let the customer know that you've been listening and to reconnect them with the notion that this is about them, not you.

For example: "Based on what you told me, I recommend that you purchase the xyz model…The way it'll help you specifically is…" And then proceed to put this scenario in their world. This is critical and can build so much extra value for you as a salesperson.

Tell your customer how it will help them by incorporating what you've learned about them during your Replaying/Exploring expeditions with phrases like:

"You mentioned earlier that…Here's then why this will work for you…"

"Remember when you said that…What this means to you is…"

"Didn't you say that you prefer…This will be important to you because…"

What I'm doing is tailoring my product/service presentation specifically for that particular customer and no one else. Make your proposal/recommendation specific and exclusive to that clients' world, and your chances for success will increase dramatically.

Many salespeople still say in their proposal/recommendation phase, "This is the number 1 brand in the country" or "ABC Company down the street uses this".

Well, if I as a customer don't mention that your product being number 1 is important or that I want to use what someone down the street is using, don't bring it up. Focus and connect it to what I expressed concern about.

During the initial exploring/interviewing session you may have discovered that a customer is more struck by delivery times or product quality. Whatever is important to the customer then, must be at the heart of your proposal/recommendation now.

Years ago I had a certificate of deposit that had matured and I went to the bank to consider my options.

I had been traveling constantly, my old car was starting to break down, and I had some money tucked away for a while and was planning on using some of the maturing cash to buy a new car.

I knew exactly which car I wanted! I had planned this for a while and the car was a reward to myself for years of hard work and constant travel.

When I met with the financial advisor at the bank I informed her that I was going to take some of the cash out of my CD and then roll the rest over. She asked me what I was going to do with the cash that I was pulling out.

Normally, I might have said, "That's my business", but she seemed nice and I always like to be nice to people so I told her, "I'm going to buy a new car!"

Her immediate response back to me was, "Oh, you don't want to do that! Let me show you some other options." I responded, "Oh, yes I do. I've been planning this for a while."

Only then did she realize that my mind had already been made up.

After a few moments she said, "Well, Mr. Kahrs, what do you do for a living anyhow?"

I indicated to her that I teach training seminars in public speaking and sales. She came back with, "So, how am I doing so far?"

Again, I'm a nice guy so I didn't have the heart to tell her.

In actuality, she had no interest in me. She wanted to serve her own agenda by getting me to invest whatever I had with her, regardless of what I personally wanted to do with the money.

She didn't take the time to explore and investigate what my real needs and wants were. I obviously did need to make some other investments and diversify my portfolio, but I did not pick her to advise me on my future investments.

Get to know your clients! It's what's at the heart of the "Consultative Toolbox Technique" process.

Closing the Sale

One of the first automotive seminars that I taught on the East Coast was for a group of managers.

We discussed employee challenges and I'll never forget one manager telling me the story about how he followed his worst salesman around for two days, trying to figure out what was wrong.

As the sales manager explained it, the salesperson in question was a nice guy, friendly, good-looking, and very bright. In fact he had an engineering degree from Brown University and could "probably build a car from scratch," as the sales manager put it.

He could not, however, figure out what the problem was and why this guy only averaged selling two cars a month.

After two days, the sales manager came to the conclusion that this salesperson never asked for the sale; he never asked for the order.

It reminded me very much of a guy that worked for me when I was a District Manager in the wine and spirits industry.

Steve was a likeable, knowledgeable guy who actually made wine at home. He knew more about brewing, distilling, and winemaking than just about anyone, but his sales where consistently low, and his accomplishments always ranked towards the bottom.

But why? Well just like the car salesperson, Steve never asked for the business.

It's interesting to note, because there does come a time when every salesperson has to ask for the business. It doesn't always come automatically.

But lets talk about different ways of closing customers and let's try to remain consultative in the process.

If the client wants to buy something, as we discussed earlier, that's fine. Just take the order and feel free to do it in a closed-ended, old-fashioned way like, "Can we do business?"

However, not all situations are that easy and many times the customer wants to feel as though they are in control of the entire process, fine!

Here are some great closes for people that feel like they need to be in control:

"What would you like me to do now?"

"So, what do you think?"

"Well…?"

"I can tell you like this model. How can I help?"

"Can you think of any other reason we shouldn't go ahead with this?"

These closes leave the decision up to the buyer and leave him or her in control of the process.

The last two are designed to smoke out or dust-bust for any other objections.

The key is to pause after you drop these phrases into dialogue. It's probably a big decision for your customer. Put yourself in their shoes. Let them take a moment to respond. Listen!

Remember what Confucius said about silence being the best companion. I couldn't agree more. Especially this close to the sale.

Naturally, there could be other challenges at this point, and if that happens, you may have to Replay/Explore some more and then try again.

What Now?

This last section of the book is about dialogue skills, not trickery. It is also not about memorizing a script. Try these skills initially in their most basic form, and just drop these various phrases into dialogue as you see fit.

You'll see how easy to use these skills actually are!

The OPIner is always a good place to start and then Rewind/Explore, Explore/Rewind whenever you feel like it, and however often it's necessary.

Don't use the same words over and over again, try different lead-in phrases to Replay, and various probes to Explore, but always be conversational and don't overuse any of these skills. Wearing out and exhausting these tools will make you suspect.

Since there's no rigid formula, simply remain flexible, and go with the flow.

What will amaze you is how easy it is to get others to talk. That's always a good thing, especially in business. Remember that you're getting smarter when you are listening, just like Columbo.

I hope these dialogue skills will help you develop your relationships and that you'll become more successful. But above all, have fun and enjoy getting to know the people you do business with.

A Final Thought

This last section of the book deals with consultative dialogue skills. If you've read this section, you probably can sense the power that these techniques have, and we've only scratched the surface.

I've included this "extra section" in the book to whet your appetite for these truly remarkable, life changing, dialogue concepts.

Again, these skills can be applied in much greater depth to all areas of business communication, including of course selling and negotiating, hiring and managing, telephone skills, business writing, and even presentation and media skills.

Also, please keep in mind that "Enhancing Your Presentations Skills" is a very useful reference piece and guidebook, but actually trying these skills with the help of a private coach is the only way that we truly learn.

Please, contact Kahrs Communication Concepts for details on all of these seminars, workshops, and keynote speeches.

Kahrs Communication Concepts
#15 Butterfly
Irvine, California
92604-1951
Telephone: (949) 551-2393
Web site:
http://thetrainer4u.com
E-mail: tillkahrs@earthlink.net
E-mail: tillkahrs@hotmail.com

Till K. Kahrs-BIO

Till K. Kahrs has been a management and communication consultant for over ten years. Kahrs has provided communication skills training for nearly half of the Fortune 500. He has shared his knowledge with literally thousands of people, training individuals from virtually every industry and background imaginable throughout the U.S., Europe (Till is fluent in German), and Asia.

Kahrs is a real performer in many respects, applying the concepts he teaches to everyday life. His experience in the entertainment industry (Till is a member of the American Federation of Television & Radio Artists-AFTRA) adds the color and vitality so necessary to teach, motivate and captivate an audience. In his first sales position, after completing college, he was promoted to District Manager within nine months, making him the youngest person to hold such a position in the entire history of the company. Thereafter, he surpassed his previous accomplishment when he became the youngest-ever Regional Manager for another Fortune 500 company.

Till, who holds an MBA, is a published author ("U.S. Sales and Marketing Strategies"), has produced and starred in many training videos, and appeared in several national TV commercials and TV shows. He has also performed many of his hit songs internationally.

This unique background allows Till to continually draw from his wide range of experience in sales, marketing, training, and the entertainment industry. His fresh perspective is what makes Kahrs Communication Concepts distinctive.

An avid tennis player, Kahrs believes in a friendly non-threatening approach to training. Like many, he feels that people learn more when they enjoy themselves. Don't expect another boring seminar or presentation from Kahrs Communication Concepts. Your audiences will be captivated, they will learn, and they won't "change the channel".

www.ingramcontent.com/pod-product-compliance
Lightning Source LLC
Chambersburg PA
CBHW030939180526
45163CB00002B/625